THE INSIDER'S GUIDE TO

B·A·L·I

THE INSIDER'S GUIDES

AUSTRALIA •BALI •CALIFORNIA •CANADA •CHINA •EASTERN CANADA •FLORIDA •HAWAII •
HONG KONG •INDIA •INDOCHINA •INDONESIA •JAPAN •KENYA •KOREA •NEPAL •
NEW ENGLAND •NEW ZEALAND •MALAYSIA AND SINGAPORE •MEXICO •
PORTUGAL •RUSSIA •SPAIN •THAILAND •TURKEY •WESTERN CANADA

The Insider's Guide to Bali
First Published 1989
Second Edition 1994

CFW Publications Ltd.
by arrangement with Novo Editions, S.A.
53 rue Beaudouin, 27700 Les Andelys, France
Telefax: (33) 32 54 54 50

© 1994 Novo Editions, S.A.

ISBN: 962 7031 44 5

ACKNOWLEDGMENTS
The Author would like to acknowledge the kind assistance given him by many people, but
particularly by Russel Farr, Gede and Budi Sudantha, Mr Oka of Puri Anyar, Kerambitan, and
Doktorandus Rai of the Badung Tourist Office, Denpasar.

Photo Credits
Leonard Lueras: Title page; pp.9 *top,* 14-15, 16-19, 24, 32–33, 34 *left*, 35 *right*,
48 *bottom*, 53, 55, 60–61, 76–77, 81, 88–89, 92–93, 96–97, 102, 135, 137, 139, 150,
151, 169, 184–185, 189, back cover *bottom right*
Rio Helmi: Front cover, pp. 20-21, 67, 80, 107, 132
Bradley Winterton, pp. 46–47, 48 *top*, 68, 173–174

Created, edited and produced by Novo Editions, S.A.
Edited by: Jude Bond
Editor in Chief: Allan Amsel
Original design concept: Hon Bing-wah
Picture editor and designer: Leonard Lueras
Text and artwork composed and information updated
using Ventura Publisher software

Printed by Samhwa Printing Company Limited, Seoul, Korea

THE INSIDER'S GUIDE TO

B·A·L·I

by Bradley Winterton

Photographed by Nik Wheeler

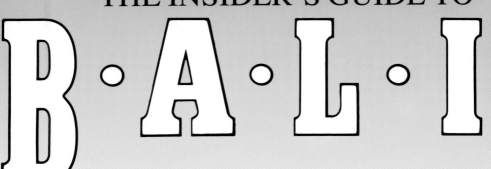

CFW GUIDEBOOKS
Hong Kong

Contents

B·A·L·I

JAVA SEA

S. Pab

Banyuwangi

Pulaki

Lovina Beach

Gilimanuk

Seririt

Cecik

Banyuwedang

Mt Kelatakan

Mt Sangiang

BALI STRAIT

Mt Mesehe

NATIONAL PARK

Candikesuma

Negara

Rambutsiwi

Prancak River

CHINA

TAIWAN

BURMA

LAOS

THAILAND

VIETNAM

CAMBODIA

THE PHILIPPINES

MALAYSIA

BORNEO

PACIFIC OCEAN

INDONESIA

Bali

AUSTRALIA

N

10 km

Pι

The Island of Bali

VOLCANOES IN THE OCEAN

Most modern geographers believe that Australia is slowly but unstoppably moving northward. It's nothing to worry about — reliable estimates put the speed of this movement at approximately equal to that of the growth of a human finger-nail. Nevertheless, the immense area of ocean floor surrounding the Australian landmass has, over the millennia, edged up against the sea bed extending south from mainland Asia, and, where they have made contact, been forced downwards and underneath it. Consequently, the edge of what the geologists call the Australian Plate now lies under the edge of the Asian one, and, as it nudges its way northward, it is forced deeper and deeper into the molten magma of the earth's inner mantle.

Owing to the phenomenal heat in the earth's depths, these slowly descending rocks have melted. In addition, movement on such a scale has caused unimaginable pressure to build up underground. Consequently this newly molten material has taken advantage of weaknesses in the earth's crust to burst through and surge upwards. The result has been, strung out along a line marking the meeting point of two continents, a chain of volcanoes, and subsequently of islands. These islands were for long known as the East Indies and are now called Indonesia.

To be accurate, not all the islands of this immense country that straddles the equator for 5,500 km (3,400 miles) and over three time zones are volcanic in origin. But Bali is. Virtually the entire island is made up of what its line of volcanoes past and present has pushed up above the waters of the Indian Ocean. Bali is its volcanoes. Two of them, Agung and Batur, have erupted this century, Batur twice. Yet despite this, Bali, like its neighbor Java, teems with people. And the reason is simple: no soil is as fertile as that produced by volcanic ash, and, with a constant supply of water for irrigation guaranteed year-round by the water-retaining

volcanic uplands and craters, the island is a rice-growers' paradise.

With over 170 million people, Indonesia is the fifth most populous country on earth, after China, India, Russia and the USA. Two and a half million live on Bali. This may not seem excessive for an island 150 km (90 miles) by 80 km (50 miles), but when you consider that the mountainous interior is very thinly populated, that the arid west almost deserted inland from the coast, and that there are no cities to speak of, this represents a considerable population density.

But then life on this favored tropical island has probably never been particularly hard. And so easy has it been for Bali's farmers to grow two crops of rice a year, there has always been time to spare for other activities. The result is Bali's celebrated dance dramas, temple festivals and generally easy-going way of life that had the early tourists from the West, back in the thirties, concluding they had at last discovered the Earthly Paradise.

AN EQUABLE CLIMATE

Bali, too, is possessed of a rather benign climate. Being just on the southern edge of the true equatorial region, it does not expe-

OPPOSITE: Part of the palace of the Rajah of Kerangasem (modern Amlapura), with Mount Agung behind. ABOVE: *Meru* at the Ulu Danu temple, Candikuning.

rience the year-long rainfall that produces the rain forests you find in the Amazon, the Congo or Borneo. Instead, Bali enjoys a long dry season, very roughly from April to October, and a shorter wet season, from November to March.

These seasons are caused by the relative heating and cooling of the great continents to the south and north of the Indonesian islands. In the Australian summer that continent becomes hotter than its surrounding seas. Hot air rises, and so winds are ultimately drawn in from the cooling continent

mum possible sunlight (and 63 percent even in January, the wettest month), so even during the rainy season skies are often clear for days on end. Furthermore, though it's often hot, temperatures never equal the levels they can reach in, for example, Greece or North Africa in summer. Cooling breezes attracted in from the sea by the high volcanoes ensure a climate where on the coast the average monthly temperature doesn't exceed 31°C (89°F), yet where the average monthly minimum never drops below 24°C (78°F). Day and night, wet season and dry,

of Asia to the north. Deflected sideways by the rotation of the earth, these winds, wet because they have crossed the seas to the north of Indonesia, become Bali's wet season northwest monsoon. By contrast, in the Australian winter winds blow northward from the cooling continent and, coming from so dry a place across a relatively narrow ocean, become the southeasterlies of Bali's dry season.

Records show that the south of the island receives annually 78 percent of the maxi-

the temperature remains warm but equable. It's a lot cooler, and with a bigger difference between day and night, up in the mountains.

What prevents the Balinese climate being ideal is the constantly high relative humidity—75 percent on average. This is the factor that can make temperatures that are not excessive in themselves at times extremely wearying.

TROPIC LANDSCAPE

The physical shape of Bali is simply a product of the forces that created it.

The volcanoes that form its central spine fall steeply to the sea in the north, leaving only a few valleys and a narrow coastal strip

Rice culture — ABOVE: Rice terraces near Ubud. The island's intricate terracing system, one of its many glories, is best seen in the center and east of the island. OPPOSITE: Rice being brought home at harvest time.

where agriculture is possible. To the south and east of the mountains, however, because the land has been lifted by the deeply burrowing edge of the Australian coastal plate, the slopes are gentler and extensive alluvial plains have been deposited. This area of very rich volcanic soils cut into by fast-flowing streams is the Balinese heartland and the site of its great kingdoms and their highly developed cultures.

The same lifting that produced lush southern Bali also raised from the sea bed the large limestone island of Nusa Penida, and the limestone peninsula south of the airport, probably also once an island, known as the Bukit.

Western Bali tapers away toward Java as the land-creating volcanoes, now it seems extinct, decrease in size.

Bali's coral reefs and silted-up estuaries have meant that the island has been without natural harbors. During the dry season the southeasterlies produce the heavy surf for which southern Bali is famous but which makes landing any kind of boat difficult, and during wet months the northwest monsoon makes access to the nearest thing Bali has to a natural harbor, at Singaraja, all but impossible. Nowadays large ships use Padangbai in the east, but even here liners have to anchor offshore and offload their passengers by lighter. Southwest Bali, however, protected by Java from the worst of the weather, is the home of the island's largest fishing fleets.

Bali's fauna and flora are very similar to Java's. The roar of the old Balinese tiger has probably been silenced now forever, even in its last refuges in remote west Bali. Similarly, crocodiles are no longer on show in the Prancak River. Wild monkeys, though, are still common, as are various kinds of bats. Turtles are regularly caught and slaughtered for temple feasts. The domesticated Balinese pig can be seen in every village, and so can the beautiful faun-like Balinese cattle. Water buffalo lug carts along the roads in the north.

Bali's forests consist of the spectacularly tall and skeletal coral tree, the erect and unbranching *pala*, teak, mahogany and, high on the mountains, pine. A sacred banyan tree stands somewhere in every village, and huge *kepuh* are frequently found growing

round cemeteries. There are several species of palm — coconut, *lontar* (providing leaves for making traditional-style books), *sago* (providing sap for palm beer, and material for thatching) and *salak* (yielding the fruit of the same name). The waxy white and yellow flowers of the frangipani spread their sweet scent around many a temple precinct.

FROM JAVA MAN TO GOLKAR

It's almost certain that originally man spread outwards from the tropical regions of the

world, and specimens of early man have been found in Java. The basic Malay-type population of modern Indonesia appears to have been there for several thousand years at least, and the evidence of the wide extent of peoples speaking Malayo-Polynesian languages points to a large ethnic group extending from peninsular Malaysia in the west eastwards to the Philippines.

To this population, with its belief in spirits that inhabit all places and all things, came Indian Hinduism, in about the second century AD. The reason isn't hard to see.

If you want to travel from India to China, and not have to cross the highest mountain ranges on the planet, you must sail south, down the coast of Burma and through the narrow Straits of Malacca that lie between peninsular Malaysia and Sumatra. Once trade became established along this route, it cannot have been long before the desire of the Indian merchants to trade with the islands, and especially with rich Java to the south, combined with the ambitions of the Sumatrans to exert some measure of control over the trade sailing past their shores to produce extensive cultural interaction. Then the natural tendency of the more complex and more highly organized culture to dominate the simpler and less sophisticated one meant that both Indian and Chinese influences on the tropical islands south of the Asian mainland began early.

Along with Hinduism, the Indian merchants and priests brought with them their whole complexly interrelated culture — Sanskrit, the caste system, and Indian mythology. Remnants of all these are still found even in Moslem Java, where the shadow puppet plays and the dance dramas continue to portray the characters of the great Indian epics.

Under these influences, and with a naturally rich soil, Java eventually produced a series of powerful Hindu, and later Buddhist, civilizations, from the Mataran to the Majapahit. Sumatra, less easy to cultivate, concentrated on the control of trade, and its Srivijaya empire too flourished. At their most extensive, the maritime trade routes stretched from China to Arabia and East Africa, and all through the Straits of Malacca. Bali, rather on the edge of things, and lacking both the natural resources and harbors of Java, joined and left empires as they waxed and waned.

These old Hindu empires, with connections as far west as Madagascar, must have been something very exotic. How far their imported culture penetrated into the lives of the ordinary people is another matter. The immense Buddhist temple at Borobodur in central Java and the nearby Hindu one at Prambanan are, however, evidence both of extraordinary dedication and exceptional powers of organization.

1. *Detroit de Baly*. 3. *Detroit de B*
2. *Cap de Porcus*. 4. *Ville de B*

An old French map of Bali. The island is seen from the north, with Java on the right and Nusa Penida to the left. The number 4 marks Denpasar — *Ville de Baly* ("Bali town").

DE BALY OU PETITE JAVA

5. Cocterius . 7. Palais du Roy. 9. Palais du Roy. 11.Plan d'un Palais du Roy.
6. Capua . 8. Coulaen . 10. Palais du Roy .

T. VIII. N.° XIII.

And just as trade with India and China had brought Hindu and later Buddhist priests to Indonesia, as well as Chinese scholars, so trade with Arabia eventually led to the arrival of Islam in the archipelago.

Everywhere along the coast of Java in the fifteenth century rajahs were becoming sultans, and the final outcome of this expansion of Islam into the region was the fall of the great Majapahit empire and the flight of its aristocracy, priesthood and community of artists and scholars across the narrow strait from east Java onto the neighboring island of Bali.

The emperor became the king of Bali and rajah of Klungkung, and the rest of the island was divided up into seven diminutive kingdoms — Bandung, Tabanan, Bangli, Gianyar, Karangasam (Amlapura), Buleleng (Singaraja) and Jembrana (West Bali) — and given to members of the ex-Majapahit royal family to rule. Men used to ruling an empire now began to focus their attention on a medium-sized island.

These Balinese kingdoms vied with one another over the centuries, first one becoming dominant, then another. But culturally, and, more important, religiously, the island was a whole. On great festival days the Balinese traveled to the Mother Temple at Besakih irrespective of the kingdom they resided in. Though there were wars between them from time to time, it seems likely these kingdoms were largely the playthings of the rajahs who ruled them. Their boundaries form the basis for the island's modern administrative districts.

Why Islam never moved into Bali as well remains something of a mystery. Islam certainly extended further east into Sulawesi and the Moluccas. The root reason is probably that the faith spread with trade, and Bali, with little to offer and no harbors, was consequently ignored.

Nevertheless, this prolonged cultural interaction has left its mark on the island. There are Moslems in the eastern-facing ports of Padangbai and Kusamba, and Buddhist priests work alongside the Hindu ones. And up in the mountains, the Bali Aga, old-style Balinese who never accepted the caste system and other imports brought in with Hinduism, continue their intransigent existence.

Thus Bali (with a section of western Lombok) became what it remains today, the only predominantly non-Islamic territory in the entire archipelago, and an isolated outpost of Indian Hindu culture gorgeously stranded in the tropical seas south of the equator.

And rather than fade away, cut off from its source, Balinese culture has flourished, apparently intact, and continues to do so today, even in the presence of an unprecedented influx of tourism and consequent Western materialism.

It could be argued that the Balinese were well trained in keeping foreign influences at bay by three hundred years of contact with the Dutch. Improved ship production brought the various European powers to the East in the sixteenth century. Acquiring spices quickly became the prime object of their expeditions; these were used not only to flavor meat but, far more importantly, to preserve it. Soon cloves, cinnamon, nutmeg and the rest were fetching staggering prices in Lisbon and Amsterdam. It was the Dutch who eventually came to dominate this immensely lucrative business and, as the British were later to do in India, soon began administering the territories they were exploiting. The former trade of what became known in Europe as the East Indies was suppressed, surplus clove trees (which threatened to lower prices in Europe) were burnt down, and the islands were made to grow an ever-increasing proportion of crops marketable back in Amsterdam. Cloves were sold for approximately 15 times the price paid for them. The old Arab-Chinese-Malay monopoly of the trade was at an end.

The Dutch first set foot in Bali in 1597, taking home glowing reports. Despite this aesthetic appreciation, the search for profits led them to Java and the eastern spice Islands of the archipelago first and foremost and, as had happened previously, Bali was ignored. If the Balinese learned any lesson from their first contact with Europeans it was probably the dangerous one that outside influence was easily deflected. The truth was the Dutch had enough on their

---

Two Balinese men at around the turn of the century. Western influence on the East Indies began early, but Bali was largely left alone because of its lack of ports and mountainous interior.

hands in the more profitable corners of the region. The trade in spices, it is true, ceased to be the license to print money it had been, and control of the islands was even temporarily lost to the British during the Napoleonic Wars when the French occupation of Holland was taken as an excuse for seizing all Dutch possessions in Asia as war booty. Nevertheless, the peace treaty saw the Dutch colonies returned, with minor adjustments, and interest in the region revived by the introduction of American cash crops such as cotton and tobacco into the islands.

One product Bali had traditionally been valued for was slaves. By the end of the eighteenth century up to two thousand Balinese were being shipped abroad annually into serfdom. The trade was finally abolished in 1830.

The nineteenth century, like the centuries before it, saw several revolts against Dutch rule. The most notable was the so-called Java War of 1825–30 where Javanese resistance was led by one Prince Diponegoro. Major streets in Denpasar and Klungkung are now named after him.

The first Dutch attempt to occupy, as opposed to keep an eye on, Bali came in 1846 when the Balinese plundering of a wreck was used as a pretext for moving in and eventually controlling the northern and western districts of the island. From then on a policy of divide and rule set the remaining Balinese kingdoms against one another until one side made the tactical error of appealing to the Dutch for assistance against its neighbors. This was what the Dutch had been waiting for and they promptly annexed the kingdom they were helping, Gianyar, in 1900.

Another instance of the looting of a wreck, this time off Sanur, led to the completion of Dutch control. This, however, did not become final until after the massacre of four thousand Balinese in Denpasar where the entire aristocracy presented itself in full ceremonial dress for ritual *puputan*, or resistance to the last man, against what were clearly superior forces. This was on September 20, 1906. A similar heroic but suicidal last stand took place in Klungkung, and then it was all over and the Dutch were masters of the whole island.

Their rule was not liked. A rigid policy of white supremacy was enforced and little was done to benefit the Balinese.

The early thirties was the time when the first Western artists began arriving in Bali, men like Walter Spies, who lived in Ubud, and Miguel Covarrubias and Le Mayeur, who settled near Denpasar and in Sanur respectively. They lived with, or at least alongside, the local people, and made a point of being independent of the Dutch administrators. They were in Bali because of the idyllic existence to be had there, in which culture and an easy life seemed to go hand in hand, and they had no use for the distinctions deemed necessary by the colonial masters for the perpetuation of their system.

Well-off tourists, too, began arriving at this time despite the difficulties and expense of travel; it's estimated that about a hundred a month were visiting Bali by the middle of the decade.

A good account of the period is K'tut Tantri's *Revolt in Paradise*. An American citizen, she settled in Bali in 1933, adopted local dress and a Balinese name, and stayed in Bali and Java until the late forties. Her book is also a good guide to the events that followed the outbreak of the Second World War.

The Japanese entered the war in 1941 and proceeded very quickly to overrun Singa-

pore, Malaya, Burma, the Philippines and
the Dutch East Indies. The Dutch colonial
army finally surrendered to them on March
7, 1942. Japanese anti-colonial propaganda
didn't win the support of the Indonesians
for long, but the opportunity was taken by
some of the emerging nationalist leaders to
advance their cause, and on the defeat of Japan
the independent Republic of Indonesia was
bravely proclaimed on August 17, 1945.

The Dutch, however, had other ideas. In
association with British forces they landed
in Indonesia with the ostensible purpose of

militant anti-Americanism, a rash "confrontation" with Malaysia and the increasing influence of the Indonesian communist party
(PKI) led to an alleged coup attempt by the PKI
on the night of September 30, 1965. This was
swiftly outmaneuvered by the army, and
since that date Major-General (now President) Suharto has been in control. Policies
have been pragmatic and pro-Western, and
the PKI has been declared illegal. A degree
of democracy has been restored but to date
the power of the ruling Golkar party has
nowhere been effectively challenged, and it

disarming and interning the Japanese
troops there. Before long, however, troops of
both nations were fighting armed Indonesian volunteers, and in November 1945 Surabaya was shelled from the sea, and bombed, by
British forces.

Eventually the British fell back on the role
of go-betweens, but the guerrilla war
against the Dutch continued until, on December 27, 1949, under international pressure, The Hague agreed to recognize the
sovereignty of the Republic of Indonesia.

The country's first president was the
long-established leader of the independence movement, Dr Sukarno (who had a
Balinese mother). He held power until the
combined effects of a declining economy,

is they and the army who essentially control
the country.

This turnabout in the nation's political
orientation was not effected, however, without a terrible purge of communists, sus-
pected communists, and, most notably, Chinese in the last months of 1965. The total
number of victims has never been agreed on
—and indeed the very account of this period
is now the subject of what ideological debate
is still permitted. In Bali alone the number
of dead almost certainly exceeded a hundred thousand, and the killing there was

ABOVE: Twentieth century colonists and visitors
recorded in stone, OPPOSITE in the temple at
Kubutambahan, North Bali.

more extensive and brutal than anywhere else in the country. According to one observer, "Whole villages, including children, took part in an island-wide witch-hunt for communists who were slashed and clubbed and chopped to death by communal consent." It's a sobering thought when considering a culture dubbed by so many as one characterized by beauty, harmony, and a serene adherence to the will of the gods.

Today Bali basks in the relative prosperity brought to it by tourism. Eighty-five percent of all Indonesia's tourists come here, and only here. For the rest, the economy remains exclusively agricultural, dominated by rice-production. The new "miracle" rice means the island now produces a surplus for export. Other exports include copra and coffee. And the Chinese are back and doing good business, in the restaurants, clothes shops and travel agencies of Kuta and elsewhere.

A NOTE ON LANGUAGE

Bali has its own language, Balinese. Though part of the Malayo-Polynesian family of languages, it's as distinct from Malay (Indonesian) as English is from German. It exists in three forms, High, Middle and Low. Lower-ranking people must use High Balinese when speaking to their superiors, but high-ranking individuals use Low Balinese when speaking to their inferiors or amongst themselves, except in very formal situations. Middle Balinese is used in delicate social circumstances.

Bahasa Indonesia, the official national language of Indonesia, is indistinguishable except in occasional words from Malay. It is taught in all schools as a part of Indonesia's government policy. Most younger Balinese can speak it when necessary.

Lastly, the ancient Javanese tongue of Kawi is used by the priests, and as the language of the gods in the shadow puppet dramas.

Bali is extraordinary in the continuance of Hinduism there thousands of miles away from its Indian home. Processions to the temple such as this one are a reasonably common occurrence.

The Culture of Bali

A VILLAGE UPBRINGING

BANJAR AND SUBAK

With the exception of the Bali Aga settlements, Balinese villages all follow a similar pattern.

The village is invariably on either side of a road. Along this road run thatched walls with somewhat higher roofed gateways, also thatched, leading into the family compounds. Side roads at right angles to the main road lead to the rice terraces, while immediately behind the family compounds are kitchen gardens where crops such as green vegetables and corn are grown.

Somewhere in the center of the village will stand the communal buildings, the village temple (pura desa), the assembly pavilion (bale agung), the kul-kul tower, and, more often than not, a sacred banyan tree.

Some way away from the village will be the village cemetery, a rough grassy field surrounded by trees where cremations take place and bodies are buried temporarily prior to cremation. A small temple of the dead (pura dalem) will also be there.

Low-bellied pigs forage freely round the village and mangy dogs hang out, despised and only half tolerated. Fighting cocks in round bamboo cages are often placed on the ground where they may be seen and admired, and where they can peck at the earth before being moved on to a new patch.

Chickens, too, wander at will, but ducks are herded daily into the rice paddies where they are kept together by means of a tall pole topped with a white cloth. For some reason the ducks never stray far from this marker.

Balinese villages are shady, well-tended places where gardens, and the communal manipulation of running water, give a strong sense of security and order.

Villages are run by a council (krama desa) of which every married householder is a member. This council elects one of its members as leader (klian desa) and meets in the bale agung. It orders the life of the village and makes arrangements for festivals. It can also administer punishment, essentially expulsion: this is very serious in Bali as, once expelled from his village, a man will find no refuge anywhere else on the island.

It isn't long before the visitor realizes that every hotel worker he comes into contact with identifies strongly with his village and hurries back there whenever he has a couple of days off, even if it's on the opposite side of the island.

Large villages and towns are sub-divided into banjar. These operate just like villages, each with its own temple, council, bale agung and the rest. In this way, village organization continues, even in the capital Denpasar. Each banjar has its own festival on its temple odalan (anniversary — see HIGH DAYS, page 41), and, on the night before Nyepi — a great all-island festival — each banjar in Denpasar parades its own lovingly made monster through the central streets without any hint of rivalry.

The Balinese aristocrats still often live in their palaces (puri), and these are sited within villages rather than outside them. These large walled compounds are like miniature villages in themselves, containing houses for different family members, each with its own garden and sub-dividing wall. There is no real middle class in rural Bali. The Chinese businessmen and the shopkeepers of Kuta, together with the other self-made people, tend to live in or just outside Denpasar.

Although various rice fields are nowadays owned by individual villagers, the old cooperative system of agriculture still continues to exist. One of the reasons for this is that irrigation has to be communal, and the flow of the water, the careful provision of exactly the right amount of water for all the fields before it is allowed to flow away downstream to the next village, requires the most careful and intricate management.

The organizations that oversee this operation are known as subak. Everyone who owns a rice field is a member. The subak meets monthly, sometimes more often, at the shrine out in the rice field dedicated to the deities of agriculture. Decisions are then made as to what repairs or improvements are needed, and who shall be responsible for carrying them out.

Rice is central to the island's life. These beautifully terraced fields have been flooded for the planting-out of the young shoots.

THE CULT OF RICE

To the Balinese, to eat is to eat rice. As elsewhere in Indonesia — which indicates the cult is pre-Hindu — the rice plant is treated as a woman, and the stages of her birth, growth, pregnancy and final fruition are all celebrated. She is Dewi Sri, the rice goddess.

First comes the laying out of the seed to germinate. This is considered worthy of a small offering and done on a propitious date by the Balinese calendars. Some 45 days later the shoots are planted out in the waterlogged paddies, first in a ritual pattern — nine seedlings in the shape of a star — then in rows one hand-span apart. Nowadays, however, such ceremonies are usually preceded by an application of trisodium phosphate, a government-recommended fertilizer.

Forty-two days later her "birthday" is celebrated with altars in the fields. When the grain first appears, Dewi Sri is said to be with child. Altars are again erected in the fields and foods that pregnant women have a taste for are presented as offerings. Rites are performed to ward off the vermin (or evil spirits) that might attack the grain.

Four months after the planting (five months for traditional strains), comes the harvest. Effigies are made of Dewi Sri and her husband Wisnu from the first sheaves and taken to the cultivator's household temple. A Rice Mother is declared and placed to oversee the harvest to the end.

The ingenuous look on the face of the little Dewi Sri figures called *cili* can often be seen in Balinese art, and in unexpected places everywhere. With their primordial simplicity, *cili* represent the impish soul of the island.

Only men plant and tend the rice, but everyone takes part in the harvest. It's a collective activity, too, and the harvesters go from one irrigation cooperative to another till the work is over.

The rice cultivated in Bali is nowadays almost exclusively the new "miracle" rice, a shorter, less elegant plant than the old rice depicted in paintings from before the seventies, but yielding at least a 50 percent larger crop, and over a shorter growing period. The older kind, however, is said to taste better and fetches a higher price than the "miracle" variety in the markets.

WHERE DO YOU SIT?

Caste is almost certainly more deeply embedded in the Balinese psyche than appears at first sight.

In the same way that the Hindu religion was brought, in the Majapahit invasion, to a people previously content with worshipping spirits of place and of their ancestors, so too the age-old Hindu distinction be-

tween people born to different roles in life was superimposed on a culture that was essentially collective and probably relatively classless. And just as the Balinese have taken to the one, so they have accepted the other. Despite the fact that 93 percent of the population has to be content with membership of the lowest of the four castes, the Sudra, they appear to accept uncritically the claims of the other three castes, and even at times, when away from their home villages, seek to adopt their status for themselves.

Some commentators have judged that caste in modern Bali represents little more than a pleasant diversion. Perhaps this is the impression the Sudras would like to give, and that the top-dog Brahmanas can afford to give (seeing as they are often also the richest people around). Nevertheless, the complexities of an intercaste marriage have not lessened with the arrival of a few hundred thousand tourists on the beaches of Kuta and Sanur.

Essentially, the Brahmanas were the priestly caste, the Satrias the warriors, the Wesias the merchants, and the Sudras the ordinary people. A long-standing struggle between the Brahmanas and the Satrias over which of them was the senior group seems to have been resolved in a de facto victory for the Brahmanas.

to the custom of always sitting lower than someone of a higher caste) remains a question strangers will often ask each other on first acquaintance.

NAMING OF NAMES

Balinese personal names usually refer to the position of the child in the family order. The first-born is Wayan — or, in the higher castes, Putu or Gede. The second is Made — or Nengah or Kadek. The usual name for the third-born is Nyoman, with Komang as an

The following titles are used by the four groups as prefixes to their names:

Brahmana Men: *Ida Bagus*; women: *Ida Ayu* (*Dayu* for short). Both these mean "high-born and beautiful."

Satrias Men: *Cokorde, Anak Agung, Ratu, Prebagus*; women: *Anak Agung Isti, Dewa Ayu*.

Wesia Men: *I Gusti, Pregusti*; women: *I Gusti Ayu*.

Sudra Men: *I*; women: *Ni*.

Legally, feudal discrimination according to caste is forbidden. And it is true that Brahmanas can be found waiting tables in restaurants and Sudras occupying reasonably important government positions. Nevertheless, socially the habits of deference persist, and "Where do you sit?" (referring

alternative. The fourth child is Ketut. These names are used for boys and girls indiscriminately. After four, the cycle is repeated, with the fifth child Wayan again and so on.

SEX ROLES

Distinction according to sex is more rigorous than that according to class.

Only men work as craftsmen (weaving excepted), climb coconut trees, tend cattle or

OPPOSITE: Weeding between the growing rice plants; note the low banks between fields and the subtly-varied water levels. Such terraces are maintained, and the water flow controlled, by close cooperation between and within villages.
ABOVE: Rice shoots waiting to be planted.

cultivate the fields (though women invariably help with the rice harvest). And only women do the housework, look after the chickens and pigs, and prepare offerings for temples.

What most surprises Westerners is to see women doing all the heavy labor on construction sites and on roadworks. The principle here is that whereas it's the men who build the traditional Balinese wooden houses, the women do the dirty work in Western-style building.

Also, it is the custom for women to carry goods on their heads, men to carry them slung at either end of a pole they carry on their shoulders. It's normally women who carry offerings to the temple, but when a man does this he too must carry them on his head.

Nevertheless, Balinese women do enjoy a measure of independence by Asian standards, keeping the profits from their economic activities for themselves and also easily obtaining a divorce from an unsatisfactory husband without incurring any serious social disapproval.

BIRTH, CHILDHOOD, LOVE AND MARRIAGE

There are few guidebooks that fail to point out that family life is particularly important to the population under discussion. Nevertheless, it does seem to be genuinely the case with the Balinese. The existence of offspring to ensure you have an adequate cremation is essential, and the more children there are to bear the cost of this expensive ceremony the better. In earlier times, and possibly still, Western contraception devices were considered akin to black magic. Failure to bear children is an acceptable ground for divorce (as is male impotence) in Balinese society.

Three months into pregnancy the mother-to-be is subject to a ceremony, and during the whole gestation period she will probably wear one or more amulets to protect her from the attention of *leyak* (witches) anxious to feed on the entrails of the unborn child. After the birth itself, the mother is

Threshing rice in North Bali. Everyone takes part in a scene that can be seen at any time of year as the climate allows crops to be planted and harvested more or less at will.

considered unclean (sebel) for 42 days (and the father for three days).

In a bizarre belief, the newborn child is considered to be accompanied by four "brothers" ("sisters" in the case of a girl), the kanda empat. These have their physical manifestation in the placenta, blood, skin-coating and amniotic fluid, all of which are saved and buried with great solemnity, the place being marked with a shrine.

It's a sign of the unequal effects of inherited beliefs on the Balinese that not so long ago the birth of twins of the opposite sex was considered as a disaster by the ordinary people, necessitating, among other things, the removal and eventual destruction of the family's house and the impoverishment of the father of the ill-begotten unfortunates. Among the upper castes, however, the twins were considered the reincarnations of two souls previously happily married, and their birth the occasion for great rejoicing. The situation probably represented the continuance of ancient Balinese beliefs among the ordinary people and the more successful dissemination of Hindu ideas among the upper classes, many of whom descended en masse on Bali in the sixteenth century from Java.

After 14 days, the newborn child is named, but it's only after 105 days (three months of 35 days each) that the child is allowed to touch the ground for the first time, the occasion being marked, not unexpectedly, with a ceremony. Another similar ceremony takes place after one complete Balinese year (210 days — see TIME PASSES BY, page 41) and in practice the two ceremonies are frequently combined on the later date to reduce the expense of the necessary feasting of guests and hiring of priests.

The Balinese allow their children to live an unusually natural life, as if carefully following the precepts of the most advanced child psychologists. They are suckled for as long as they want, often over three years, and allowed to feed — just like their parents — whenever they're hungry. They are held in permanent bodily contact with either the mother or another woman of the family for every moment of the first three months of life, and throughout early childhood fathers cuddle or carry their children almost as often as their mothers. Not surprisingly, Balinese children rarely cry.

Once they're able to walk, the children live a free and easy life in the village in the company of other children of their own age. They are never beaten, and little in adult life is hidden from them so that they appear to enter the world of sex at adolescence without surprise, guilt or neurosis.

Sexual relations between Balinese teenagers are left to proceed in a natural way without interference from the parents, at least in the Sudra class that makes up the vast majority of the population, and there's no expectation that early affairs will necessarily lead to marriage. Love charms and magically potent amulets are often used when the girl seems reluctant. Homosexuality is frowned on but seems rare.

The relaxed attitude to sex goes on to apply to marriage. Parents have a minimal part to play in the arrangements, and in the commonest form of marriage the ceremony doesn't take place until several days after the announcement of consummation. And even in upper-caste "arranged" marriages, the couple may sleep together for an agreed period before the wedding.

The commonest form of marriage in Bali is by kidnapping (ngrorod). The boy seizes the girl in some public place and, after token resistance, the couple speed off to a prearranged hidey-hole where offerings are set out for the gods and the union consummated. It's considered vital this happens before the offerings wilt in order for the union to be valid. This is the real marriage, performed in the sight of the gods, and the subsequent public celebration is merely a recognition of an already-achieved actuality.

Arranged marriages (mapadik) are commonest among the aristocracy, but only with the full agreement of both parties.

The wedding ceremonies take place at the home of the boy's father. A tooth-filing ritual (see next entry) will be incorporated if this operation hasn't been performed already. There's much feasting and music, but the actual ceremony is a simple one with the priest just blessing the union amid much throwing of flowers, ringing of bells and dashing with holy water.

Girl taking an offering to the temple. Under a very free system of child-rearing, the Balinese mature early and retain a natural dignity throughout adult life.

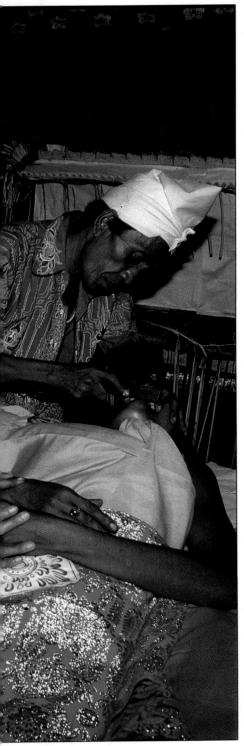

A Balinese woman couldn't in the past normally marry a man of lower caste than herself, a prohibition that merely echoed the attempts of the rich everywhere to try to make sure their daughters don't descend the social scale when they marry. If this is changing nowadays, it's changing slowly. Marriage with divorcees and widows, however, is freely allowed.

Balinese women can divorce their husbands — for cruelty, impotence or failure to support them — by simply walking out of the house. The divorce is then confirmed by the village council; this is generally a formality as there are no set criteria by which "support" or "cruelty" can be judged.

TOOTH-FILING

It is considered essential for every Balinese adult sooner or later to have his or her teeth filed — so much so that in the event of accidental death in youth the teeth of the body will be filed before cremation.

The purpose of the ceremony is to reduce the power of the vices of greed, jealousy, anger, drunkenness, lust and "confusion" that are considered more appropriate to animals than to humans. Consequently, the two upper canine teeth, and the four incisors between them, are filed down amid feasting and general celebration. Because of the cost of the hospitality involved, tooth-filing ceremonies are often held in conjunction with other rituals. And because it's thought desirable to have had your teeth filed before you get married, the ceremony is frequently held in conjunction with a wedding.

Ideally, the six teeth are filed down by someone of the Brahmana cast, perhaps the upper-caste patron of the family concerned. The patients, dressed in their finest, lie down in a pavilion, usually two at a time, surrounded by offerings. They are then wrapped in a white cloth while family and friends gather round.

Tooth-filing — this curious custom is still rigorously observed by all Balinese, and no young man or woman can be married before the ceremony has been completed. Groups of adolescents often have their teeth filed together, and marriage and tooth-filing rituals frequently take place together.

The extent to which the teeth are filed down depends largely on the wishes of the subject, but as filed teeth are considered beautiful as well as an aid to virtue, it's not uncommon for a thorough job to be requested. The filing usually takes between 15 and 30 minutes. The mouth is held open by a short piece of sugar-cane and from time to time the patient spits out the filings into a yellow coconut which is later buried in the family temple. A small mirror allows the victim to inspect the work and request improvements. Often hundreds of young men and women have their teeth filed together in one ceremony to save on expense.

MEN AND GODS

BALINESE HINDUISM

Every Balinese will describe himself to you as a Hindu, but the truth of the matter is that the elements of Hinduism found in Bali are rather like the Catholicism found in the remoter parts of the Philippines. For some it

The charm of the Balinese is the charm of a people whose natural grace has been sustained and augmented by a religion that is based on respect and reverence for the life of all things.

may be a genuine presence, and its philosophy a real foundation for faith and action, but for the majority it is a dressing applied to the more fundamental and essential spirit-religion found everywhere in the Malay archipelago.

Nevertheless, it is an extraordinary phenomenon to find, isolated on one south-sea island, manifestations of a religion originating somewhere near the Caspian Sea and brought into north India nearly four thou-

sand years ago. Even then the tenets of Hinduism were far from new. The origins of the Vedas, the holy books of the Aryans who brought Hinduism to India, are lost in the mists of antiquity, but the oldest of them, the Rig Veda, is certainly the oldest religious text known anywhere in the world.

And the central tenets of Hinduism do fit in very well with a system of beliefs that holds that the world is everywhere populated by spirits. A people who believed from the start that in every bush, volcano, fortunate or disastrous event there was an invisible intelligence at work cannot have found it difficult to take to a philosophy that taught of a World Soul of which we, and all other living things, are temporary embodiments.

To the educated Hindu, the whole universe is ordered by a controlling spirit, Brahman. Your inner essence, the silent core of your being that remains when all the lusts for money, sex and power are stilled, is your Atman. And the innermost secret, the core of the mystery, is that the two, your "soul" and the vast spirit of the universe, are one and the same thing. You are a part of it, manifested for a brief time in matter. So is a mouse, a tree, a grain of corn.

The cycle of birth and death, creation and destruction, goes on forever, the essence of all things constantly embodying itself in matter. And in just the same way that all things are part of the great World Spirit, so their death is no tragedy, merely the returning of the part to the whole, a whole from which innumerable new manifestations will be born.

This constant rebirth of the spirit, at a higher or lower level of creation according

to the place your acts have brought you to in your last incarnation, is natural and inevitable. But it's wearisome to the high-aspiring soul who longs for permanent rest, for final union with the creating spirit itself. And because the spirits of all things and the great universal spirit are essentially one and the same, this ultimate union, or reunification, is possible. Reject all desire, which holds you down among the world of mate-

rial things, and you might attain that final fusion with the ineffable and unimaginable that is known as *moksa*. You at last realize the potential that has been in you all along and become one with Brahman.

No philosophy could be more remote from Western materialism where competitiveness, greed, and the desire to conquer nature (rather than realize one's true part in it) are implied in the cult of individualism and the right, above all, to "be yourself."

This is the philosophic heart of Hinduism and, over the millennia, innumerable less pure manifestations of it have grown up in India and elsewhere, just as Christianity has seen the veneration of relics and the endless matching of texts from the Bible. So, in Bali, orientation of temples toward the volcanoes and the use of cock's blood (obtained at cock-fights) in temple rituals seem remote from the pure spirituality of the Chandogya Upanishad. People everywhere seem to need to see and touch, to develop local sanctities and hold on to the practices of their ancestors. But the heart of the matter lies elsewhere.

Even so, the influence of the great Hindu vision is remarkably pervasive. Balinese cremations really are genuinely cheerful affairs, and the numerous rituals preceding

them and symbolizing the cutting off of attachment to the soul of the dead man or woman are living parts of ordinary village life. The soul must be allowed to go free, and not be held back by grief — so teaches the religion; and the result is, remarkable as it may seem, the ordinary Balinese at a cremation do not mourn. Despite all the animist belief in spirits and blood sacrifice, the essence of Indian Hinduism has entered into the people's souls.

Nevertheless, the variety of religious practice, the number of places and things that can be venerated, is astonishing. There's hardly a field, a large tree, a shop or even a discotheque on the island that doesn't have its incense-burning shrine. The same is true, it might be argued, of Hong Kong or Bangkok, but in Bali the constant attention to these household shrines, and the frequency and elaborateness of the various temple festivals, are unparalleled anywhere.

Every village (desa) has its temple of origin (pura puseh), its temple of the dead (pura dalem), its temple for the irrigation system (pura subak), and any number of temples and shrines dedicated to local streams, lakes, springs, hills and waterfalls. All these must have their offerings on their holy days. In addition, evil spirits, thought to occupy their own special sites, but especially crossroads, must be placated with offerings too, thrown down casually and quickly crushed by the first passing car (but not before the greedy spirits have wolfed up their meager essence).

Thus the spirits of goodness are constantly being invited down into the world of everyday life, and feted at festivals, and the evil spirits kept at bay by what amount to derisory, but regular, bribes.

To the Balinese, the volcanoes are the seat of the gods. Every structure in Bali is to some extent influenced by this sense of "to the mountains" (kaja) being pure and the opposite direction (kelod) being impure. So, a house will have its shrine in its most kaja corner, and its pig-pen and garbage tip in its most kelod.

This doesn't mean that to the Balinese the sea is impure, though some Western writers have inferred this. It is true the Balinese historically have not been seafarers, but the sea itself is seen as a purifying element, used for cleansing symbolic items from the temple (arca) and one source of holy water.

These mountain-oriented temples of Bali often have a deserted, even shabby look. They contain no idols, and no priests are in attendance. Only the temple keeper (pemangku) is usually somewhere around, dressed in white, to keep the place tidy and accept the donations of visitors. On festival days, though, things are very different.

The principal festival of any temple is its anniversary (odalan), occurring every 210 days from the date of its founding. Then bamboo altars and tables are put up, and offerings of fruit, cakes and flowers, piled high on the heads of the women, are brought from the nearby houses. The pemangku receives them, pours holy water onto the hands of the villagers and places grains of rice on their temples and brow. The villagers take flower blossoms and, holding them between the tips of their fingers, raise them to their foreheads three times before throwing them toward the shrines.

The high caste priests (pedanda) are said to be the direct descendants of the Indian brahmins who officiated in the old courts of Java. They only attend temple ceremonies on the most important occasions, such as aristocratic weddings, at which they sit on a high platform ringing their bells and reciting their mantras. They can be either Buddhist or Hindu (pedanda bodda or pedanda siwa), the former going bare-headed with long hair, the latter wearing a gold and red miter crowned with a crystal ball. The chief use of these learned pedanda as far as the ordinary people are concerned is to make the holy water used in all temple ceremonies.

At these temple anniversary festivals male and female figures, the arca, made of sandalwood, or of old Chinese coins (kepeng), are deemed to symbolize the gods and are taken during the day to a river or the sea and symbolically washed. In addition, cockfights are sometimes staged in the afternoon. Gamelan orchestras play, and dance dramas may be performed. As the evening

Traditional life goes on even in the midst of the tourist invasion — a purification ceremony at Kuta. (See also next page).

wears on, coffee and cake are offered to everyone present, and certain villagers will go into a trance (during which they may also perform a sword dance) and a spirit, it is believed, will speak through them and report on how the offerings have been received by the gods.

At dawn, the women will dance in honor of the rising sun and the elaborate offerings, their essence judged to have been devoured by the gods, will be taken back home and eventually eaten by the weary devotees.

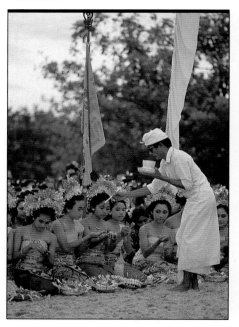

HOTELS FOR THE GODS

Walk into any Balinese temple and you'll find the same mixture of diversity and similarity you find in many Christian churches. A typical Balinese temple might present itself to you as follows.

You pass from the street into the first, or outer, compound through two carved stone structures, the inside (facing) walls of which, however, have been left smooth. The general

Purification ceremony on Kuta Beach.
ABOVE: A *pemangku* distributes holy water.
RIGHT: Facing the ocean, the devotees venerate a temporary bamboo shrine. Such ceremonies take place after, for example, a cremation.

effect is of a structure, tapering upwards, that has been split down the middle. This split gateway is known as a *candi bentar*.

This first compound is spacious and rather empty. It does, however, contain a white-clad *pemangku* who asks you to sign a visitors' book and pay a donation of a couple of hundred rupiahs.

The compound does contain some ordinary-looking pavilions (roofs resting on four posts, with a waist-level floor) and a brick tower. Climb the tower and you will find hanging at the top some hollowed

out tree trunks with slits cut into them: these are *kul-kul*, and they are hammered in times of emergency to call the villagers into the temple compound. The pavilions are used by the *gamelan* orchestras, and for preparing offerings and cooking food, on festival days.

In this hypothetical temple, there is no second outer compound. If there were it would simply contain further pavilions.

At the top end of this outer court, straight in the direction of the mountains, there is a wall with a door in it. The surrounds of the door are very ornate, and the door itself intricately carved. It's called the *padu raksa*. The door stands half open, so you climb the few steps up to it and walk through. You can't go straight ahead, however, as a short wall, an *aling-aling*, bars your way. It's actually meant to bar the way of evil spirits which are thought to travel in straight lines, as well as to be rather stupid — seeing their way barred, it's hoped, they'll reverse direction and fly back out again. You, however, turn left or right and go down the steps into the inner courtyard. You are now in the holiest part of the temple.

There are a considerable number of shrines along two walls, either the eastern and northern walls in South Bali or the eastern and southern walls in North Bali, as the

instance — communally owned by the villagers and occasionally used in festivals.

Situated in the corner between north and east in South Bali or south and east in North Bali is a stone throne placed at the summit of an elaborately carved stone structure. This is the *padmasana*, the chair for Ida Sanghyang Widhi Wasa, the supreme deity in the Balinese pantheon. The support for the chair is carved to represent the world as imagined in Balinese mythology, mountains supported by a turtle entwined with snakes. When there are three chairs instead

shrines must face the mountains. Some of these shrines are small structures a couple of meters high, little more than high-level tables with roofs of black thatch (*ijuk*). Others, though, are high towers with multiple roofs. These are known as *meru*, and the roofs are always of an odd number. The number signifies which deity they are dedicated to, as follows: 3 — Dewi Sri (rice goddess), 5 — Isawa (one of Siwa's reincarnations), 7 — Brahma, 9 — Wisnu, 11 — Siwa. The finest *meru* in Bali can be seen at Besakih and Mengwi.

Close to the eastern wall there is a rather sounder structure with locked doors. This is the *gedong pesimpanan* and contains various dusty items — masks for *barong* dances, for

of one, they are for the godhead in the form of the trinity Siwa, Wisnu and Brahma.

TIME PASSES BY

The Balinese make use of three independent calendars, a traditional Javanese calendar based on 210-day cycles, an ancient South Indian lunar calendar, and the Western — and now international — Gregorian calendar.

The old Java calendar is the basis for the calculation of the dates of all temple anniversary festivals, all of which consequently recur every 210 days. This period of time is made up of thirty weeks of seven days each — but also, superimposed on them, a whole

string of other "weeks" of one, two, three, four, five, six, eight, nine and ten days each. As not all these numbers multiply exactly to 210, various extra days of the week of the four-, eight- and nine-day weeks are discreetly added at fixed points in the cycle so that all the weeks can come to an end together on the 210th day.

The result of this system is that any particular day has ten different day-of-the-week names. In practice, however, it is only the three-, five- and seven-day weeks that interest the Balinese. These, though, are very im-

portant, and special coincidences between their cycles are used as auspicious days for ceremonies and rituals. For instance, when the third day of the three-day week coincides with the fifth day of the five-day week, it's a good day for just about anything.

Used in conjunction with this calendar (called, by the way, *pawukon*) is the lunar system known as the *saka* calendar. Being based on the moon, this calendar features months, *sasih*, each of thirty days. Each month is deemed to begin on the day following the first appearance of the new moon

The phenomenon of "possession" — men going into a trance during a temple festival. While they are "possessed", they can endure extremes of pain without apparent ill effects.

(tilem). Halfway through each month, of course, is the full moon, *purnama*. The 12 months are named after the Sanskrit words for one to ten, with names derived from other sources for the last two.

The innumerable possibilities offered by the combinations of these two systems are not lost on the Balinese, and the inter-chiming of these celestial rhythms is no doubt as much a manifestation of serious play, of variations within an overall unity, as the shifting rhythms and sudden harmonies of the *gamelan* orchestra. Life to the Balinese, at least in theory, is in large part the observing of earthly rhythms, and harmonies that reflect imagined — and possibly actual — heavenly ones.

HIGH DAYS

The commonest as well as the most important temple festivals are the ones that celebrate the *odalan* or anniversary of the temple. The majority of these are calculated according to the *pawukon* calendar which operates on a cycle of 210 days. Below are the dates of the first day of the *pawukon* cycle up to the end of the century:

> June 27, 1993
> January 23, 1994
> August 21,1994
> March 19, 1995
> October 15, 1995
> May 12, 1996
> December 8, 1996
> July 6, 1997
> February 1, 1998
> August 30, 1998
> March 28, 1999
> October 24, 1999

The festival days of a few of the major temples of Bali are listed below. The number before the temple name indicates the day in the *pawukon* calendar on which its festival occurs. Thus Bangli's Pura Kehen, having the number four, will have its festival in 1997 on July 9, the fourth day of the *pawukon* cycle which begins in that year on July 6.

4 — Pura Kehen, Bangli.

59 — Pura Ulun Danau, Chandikuning (Bedugul).

60 — Pura Bukit Sari, Sangeh (Monkey Forest).

84 — Pura Taman Pule, Mas (three-day *odalan*).

85 — Pura Sakenan, Serangan (Turtle Island).

88 — Pura Tanah Lot.

94 — Pura Taman Ayun, Mengwi (three-day *odalan*).

94 — Pura Luhur, Uluwatu.

Certain major temple festivals are fixed according to the lunar, *saka*, calendar. All the following are held at full moon, *purnama*, in one of the two months indicated — to find out more specifically, contact the Badung Tourist Office.

February/March — Pura Penataran Sasih, Pejeng.

March/April — Pura Batu, Kintamani.

March/April — Pura Besakih.

September/October — Pura Panataran Agung, Besakih.

September/October — Pura Tirtha Empul, Tampaksiring.

October/November — Pura Kehen, Bangli.

October/November — Pura Jagat Nartha, Denpasar (the state temple next to the museum).

The Badung Government Tourist Office in Denpasar publishes every month a list of imminent temple festivals, large and small, throughout the island.

THREE FESTIVALS

Nyepi celebrates the solar New Year for Bali. Despite Bali's being in the southern hemisphere, it's a sort of spring clearing-out of bad spirits. On the day before Nyepi, evil spirits are attracted down with special offerings, then terrified out of their wits as night falls by a veritable orgy of firecrackers dropped in garbage cans, gongs, beating of *kul-kul*, yelling and the parading through the streets of gigantic, hideously grotesque monsters. It's a great night to be in the streets of Denpasar and shouldn't on any account be missed.

Entrance of the *rangda* mask for a temple dance. Almost all Bali's dances are religious in origin, the only exceptions being those evolved in modern times for the benefit of foreign visitors to the island.

Nyepi is celebrated on the day after the new moon of the ninth Balinese lunar month, a date that usually falls in March.

The next day, Nyepi itself, the entire island stays home. Even tourists aren't allowed onto the beaches, or indeed out of their hotels. It's very strictly observed, and after dark bands of vigilantes throw stones through any window where a light is visible.

The idea behind it all is, however, charmingly innocent. Most of the evil spirits having been driven out the night before, on the Holy Spring at the temple of Tirta Empul at Tampaksiring, the *odalan* or anniversary festival of which is on the same day. The day after Kuningan there is a festival on Turtle Island (Serangan).

A VILLAGE CREMATION

It's a hot morning. A tour organizer wakes you early and you set off, down a road, then another, down a lane, down a track and you're there.

A high bamboo tower and a bamboo bull,

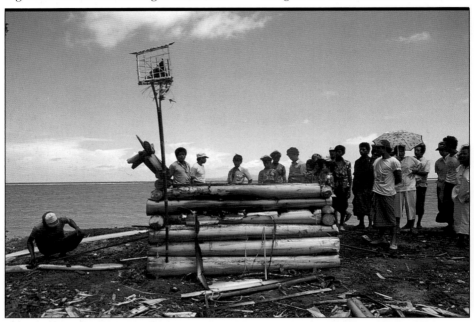

Nyepi itself a show is made of the island being totally uninhabited. It's hoped all remaining spirits will give up and fly off somewhere more congenial.

Galungan, and the festival which follows it ten days later, **Kuningan**, are celebrated every 210 days, like the temple anniversary festivals, and so can occur at any time of the year. Galungan is the time when the spirits of the ancestors return and revisit the homes of their offspring. *Barong* (giant monsters in masks) roam the streets and everything is brushed clean, dance dramas of great length are performed, and a party atmosphere prevails everywhere.

Kuningan, by contrast, is a festival of purification and is closely associated with richly adorned and shining in the early morning light, are standing ready in an open space in the middle of a village. Under a blue and orange canopy, the special cremation *gamelan*, the *gambong*, is already playing its old-style instruments, bamboo-keyed and struck by players holding four hammers apiece. You engage a young man in conversation.

The dead man was his grandfather. Aged sixty, he'd died 12 days ago in the hospital. They'd waited for an auspicious date for the cremation — there are maybe two in a month. This cremation, together with the ceremonies beforehand, will cost the family US$3,000; they'd had to feed the whole village since the day of his death.

An elegantly dressed man comes out from the nearby lodgings. He's wearing sarong, waistband, headdress and tennis shoes. He photographs the bull and, by means of an attached string, tweaks its extremely virile phallus. Great laughter from the *gambong* players. He proceeds to photograph the various groups of villagers present. The tower *(wadah)* can have anything from one to eleven roofs, like the temple *meru*. This has seven. The number, always odd, depends on the caste of the deceased (see page 39).

Everyone is dressed in their best, even "Kuta Beach" T-shirts so long as they're neat and new-looking.

The bull is moved forward, and a bamboo ramp placed against the tower. Young men in white headbands do the work. The *gambong* music becomes more excited. Women go up the ramp and rub their hair on the bier.

A procession of women carrying offerings on their heads leaves the lodgings and lines up in front of the bull. Little waves to friends in the crowd. Then they process off down the track to the intersection with the lane.

The music gets more frantic as the young men go into the lodgings; the *gambong*, previously playing in two sections, is now playing together. The odd cigarette is being smoked. One well-dressed woman comes out of the lodging carrying a plastic shopping-bag and takes up a position by the musicians.

Expectant silence now from the *gambong*. Smiles in the sunlight. Some laughter.

Two live chicks are brought out from the lodging and placed in the tower — then a long white cloth is unwound from the lodging doorway to the ramp, followed by some sausage-like bundles. The music has now resumed and is vigorous and strong.

The bull is lifted off the ground and sets off on the shoulders of the youths. There's some argument, then it's turned round and bounced up and down. Someone has the job of jigging the genitals with the string.

Suddenly the body emerges. It's wrapped in white at the end of the sheet, and it's bundled quickly into the tower, just under the lowest roof. The *gambong* is now ringing out as the cloth is wound up and stuffed into the tower at great speed.

Away down the track, at the junction with the lane, the bull is being rather wildly bounced and circled around. The body is tied securely into the tower with string. A man climbs onto the tower carrying a bird on a stick. The ramp's removed.

Bearers lift the tower, and immediately run round and round in a circle with it, laughing as they go.

And off you go, with the musicians carrying cymbals, gongs and drums walking in front of the tower. Down the track and left into the lane. Everyone follows, the old men

with the little children (the young men are all assisting at the ceremony). The sun goes in.

You pass along the lane, past paddy fields reflecting the now dull sky. School children dressed in white are formally lined up with their teachers to witness the event. Great red flowers like gladioli glow in the hedgerows. Several immobilized motorcyclists wait on the verge for you to pass. Peo-

Cremations can take place in the most public places. OPPOSITE and ABOVE: A simple cremation on the beach at Sanur. A cremation in Bali is a comparatively joyful occasion as the spirit of the dead person is being released from earthly ties and become free to reincarnate into a higher form of existence.

ple chat quietly among themselves as you walk along.

Tourists walk with the villagers. No one seems to mind them being there — if anything, they seem honored.

Finally you are there, and the tower is rushed into the rough field surrounded by high trees that is the burial and cremation place. The man on the tower throws grain on anybody within range. The tower's set down, and the ramp moved up to it.

The two chicks are untied, chirruping wildly. There's much argument as the body's half moved out and the white cloth unwound.

Clearly this is a much-used site. Burned straw lies around, and little bamboo shrines stand precariously. The *gambong* sets up, and strikes up again.

The body of the bull — a tree trunk with a lid cut into it — is opened up to receive the corpse, which is brought across and placed on top of the bull, supported on bamboo poles. The musicians stop playing. All but a few strips of stained cloth are removed. A sour aroma drifts across the grass. The bamboo poles are removed and the body slowly lowered into the wooden sarcophagus.

A lengthy wait now as the family and a priest sprinkle holy water and place items inside the bull. The people wait, chatting quietly and smoking their clove cigarettes. A drink seller toots his bicycle horn. It's like an English village fete, sociable, and pleasant and relaxed. This final placing-in of offerings is rather drawn-out. The penultimate, in life as in art, is always long.

Finally the cloth goes in, the *gambong* strikes up, and the lid is replaced in the bull's back. Plastic tubes are unwound, attached to blackened metal burners.

But the lid's removed again. The contents of the bull are checked, and a woman's making a point. Then everything's replaced and the lid put back on. The burners are put underneath and the taps opened. Kerosene (paraffin) begins to spring onto the bull and is lit by a match.

The "Village Cremation" described in the text. These days the fire is largely kerosene sprayed onto the bier from a portable tank. The actual cremation takes place at a "burning ground" just outside the village.

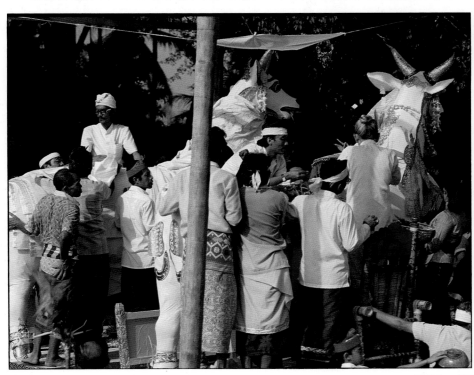

The burning is strangely non-ritualized, a technical problem. The *gambong* doesn't play. The work is done by two men in yellow plastic safety helmets.

The fire spits and roars. The body shifts position. There are explosions, bones cracking. The cloths are now burnt and the dead man grimly visible. The people are very quiet.

Then suddenly the musicians start up again, lively and even cheerful. The people relax, and your tour driver comes across and says it's time to be off.

What about the ceremony by the sea? Tomorrow. And the burning of the tower? Also tomorrow (actually later that day, but the driver wants his lunch).

And that was it.

How It Is

Bodies are often buried for some considerable time before what's left of them is exhumed for cremation. If a Balinese dies far from home, or at sea, an effigy is usually burnt in the village cemetery as a better-than-nothing substitution for the cremation proper.

The bamboo *wadah* is decorated with colored paper, tinsel, cotton ornaments and small mirrors. Sudras are entitled to only one roof, but are usually cremated in large groups, victims of the cut-price even in death. Three to eleven are reserved for the three senior castes, while a brahmanic priest or priestess has no roof at all but an empty chair akin to a temple *padmasana*. The tower and the bull are rotated frequently, and especially at crossroads, both to deceive the evil spirits and to prevent the soul of the deceased finding its way back home again. The giant head on the back of the more splendid towers is called a *bhoma*, a fanged monster with wings outstretched, decorated in colored cotton.

In the case of high-caste cremations — the kind that visitors to Bali are almost invariably taken to — there will be elaborate ceremonies too on the previous day. A procession bearing effigies *(adegan)* of the deceased will go to the house of the high priest to receive his blessing. There will be *baris* dances (see DANCE AND DRAMA, p. 58) and singing in Sanskrit, together with various small ceremonies in which members of the family symbolize their breaking of emotional ties with the dead man, ties that might otherwise hold him back in this world and keep his soul from the freedom it so desires.

In the evening prior to the cremation there will be shadow puppet performances or displays of the *barong landong* dance.

The actual burning usually takes around three hours, during which time the family goes home to rest. When they return to the cremation ground in the late afternoon it is for a more private, small-scale ceremony. The ashes have now been gathered and placed in a yellow coconut. They are taken in procession to a local river, or to the sea, and are there scattered on the water after another brief ritual.

MAGIC AND WITCHCRAFT

The Balinese won't talk about it much but they all believe in witches. Certain people become witches *(leyak)* by undergoing a series of rituals, reciting mantras backwards and the like, and the disembodied spirits of these people can be seen as green lights hovering in graveyards or at crossroads, or as animals encountered in the dark.

Though these beliefs certainly have their origins in the pre-Hindu past, they nevertheless are embraced by the Hindu world view. Negative forces are simply the opposites of the positive ones used by the temple priests. Each is a part of existence, and security is best safeguarded by ensuring a balance between the two natural sets of forces. It's the left and right of the shadow puppet plays in another form.

Most Balinese drama originates in temple ceremony (just as Western drama originated in religious performances in ancient Greece), and these dramas often involve possession, or are staged as exorcism rituals. What appears to the Western observer as "culture" is actually spiritual, not only in its origin but in present-day significance to the participants.

Whether it's a performance of the *barong* dance, the provision by a *balian* (herbal-

ABOVE: "Suddenly the body emerges. It's wrapped in white at the end of the sheet, and it's quickly bundled into the tower" (see page 45).
BELOW: cremation bulls.

ist/witch doctor/faith healer) of an amulet against illness, or the rituals surrounding *kanda empat* (see BIRTH, CHILDHOOD, LOVE AND MARRIAGE, page 29), life in Bali proceeds according to very different tenets than those the writers of the tourist brochures would have you believe.

HEROES AND VILLAINS

Ideally, anyone hoping to come to grips with Balinese culture on a serious level ought to read something of the great Indian romance, the *Ramayana*, beforehand. This is rather like saying a visitor to England should read *A Christmas Carol* or *Hamlet*, and whereas this too would undoubtedly be a good idea, it's unlikely many visitors, even those with cultural aspirations, will actually take the trouble.

Nevertheless, the ancient Sanskrit poems, the *Ramayana* and the *Mahabharata*, do still have a very pervasive influence on the Balinese, even though not one in ten thousand will have read a single line of them. Reading isn't the main means of cultural transmission in Asia, and even the epics themselves were passed on for millennia by recitation before they were ever written down. And in Bali today it is through the shadow puppet plays and the dance dramas that the people make contact with these ancient symbolic stories. It's comparable to the Middle Ages in Europe where few read the scriptures but everyone followed the religion and knew the stories of Adam and Eve, Abraham and Isaac, David and Goliath, Noah's Ark, and the birth and death of Jesus through church festivals, street dramas, paintings and stained-glass windows.

As the average visitor is only in Bali for a short time, and the shadow plays (for instance) will be in several incomprehensible languages, it will perhaps be useful to give a very brief description of these two great works, and the crucial episodes returned to time and time again by Balinese dancers and shadow puppeteers.

The *barong* dance at Batubulan (see page 62). This good-natured monster overcomes the powerful *rangda* in ritual conflict, with a little bit of help from his friends. This popular dance is really an exorcism ritual aimed at limiting the power of the *rangda*, a kind of witch.

The *Ramayana* (*The Romance of Rama*) is an immensely long poem, 48,000 lines, completed probably around 300 BC by one Valmiki, a sage who himself appears as a character in the poem.

Prince Rama, the perfect ruler and an incarnation of Vishnu (Wisnu in Bali) wins Sita to be his wife by bending the bow of the god Shiva (Siwa in Bali) at a tournament. Rama is heir to the throne of the kingdom of Ayodhya but is disinherited and forced into exile in the forest with his wife and his half-brother Laksmana.

One day, while Rama and Laksmana are pursuing a golden deer, the demon king Ravana (who has sent the deer specifically to distract Rama) seizes Sita and carries her off to his island kingdom of Lanka.

But Rama is helped by the forest monkeys, by their king Sugriva and especially by their warrior-general, the white monkey Hanuman. It's he who discovers where Sita is and leads Rama to her. In the inevitable battle that follows, Rama wins back Sita, and also, by and by, his own throne.

But the people suspect poor Sita of infidelity to Rama while she was on Lanka, and Rama is forced to place her in a hermitage. There she gives birth to Rama's twin sons and meets the sage Valmiki.

Eventually, when her sons are grown up, Sita is accepted back by the people and by Rama, but, weary of life, asks the earth to take her, which it duly does.

Already, from this brief outline, many Balinese echoes are apparent. There's a *losmen* called Ayodhya at Lovina, there's a statue of Hanuman at the entrance to the Monkey Forest at Sangeh, and the story of Rama and the deer is at the heart of the Ramayana Ballet dance.

If the *Ramayana* is long, the *Mahabharata* is positively sprawling. It's three times the length of the Old and New Testaments of the Bible put together, 200,000 lines of Sanskrit verse. And, like the Bible, it is in fact a storehouse of the history, laws, poetry and moral principles of an entire people. It was probably only revised by its supposed author, one Vyasa, any time between 400 BC and AD 400. Its title means *The Great Epic of the Bharata Dynasty*, and it's the longest poem known anywhere in the world.

The main channel in this vast and complex river of words is the story of the feud between the rival branches of a royal family, the Pandavas and the Kauravas.

Who should rule has been rendered unclear by the eldest son of the previous generation being passed over for the succession because he's blind, and then the next in line giving up the throne to become an ascetic and the blind son being brought back to rule. On his death, his five sons are forced to flee the court and go into exile, together with the wife they all share, Draupadi. They are

joined by their cousin Krishna. Eventually they return, but are forced to flee a second time when the eldest brother loses everything in a dice game with his cousin.

War becomes inescapable, and battle rages for 18 days on the field of Kuruksetra, north of modern-day Delhi. Only seven individuals survive the immense conflict, among them the five brothers and Krishna.

Krishna is later shot, mistaken for a deer, and the five brothers set out to seek the

OPPOSITE: The figure of an official in the *barong* dance. The courts of the old Hindu rajahs of Java and Bali have left their mark on a number of Balinese dramas. ABOVE: Balinese dancers' costumes are made and maintained with an extraordinary care and attention to detail.

heaven of Indra in the company of a dog, really the god Dharma in disguise. Only the eldest, Yudhisthira, eventually completes the quest.

Part of Book Six of the *Mahabharata* is the celebrated "Bhagavadgita" ("Song of the Lord"). It's a dialogue between Arjuna, one of the Pandava brothers, and Krishna before the battle. Anticipating the terrible destruction that is certain to take place, Arjuna asks if it is really right that he should fight to kill his own kith and kin in this way. Krishna replies with the doctrine of the disinterested discharge of one's duty, and in the process reveals himself as a reincarnation of the god Vishnu.

But the "Bhagavadgita," far from endorsing a militaristic ethic, goes on to encompass the heart of Hindu belief as to the nature of God, and the means of approach for the awakened soul to this supreme reality.

What is notable about the poem as a whole is the way it manifests the values of a warrior society, and then proceeds to add to these religious values that finally supersede the heroic ones and even point the way forward to the later Indian principles of non-violence and philosophical pacifism.

The stories contained in these two poems spread alongside Indian religion east into Cambodia and south to what is now Indonesia. That incidents from these epics are still so alive, and so popular, not only in India itself (where they form the material for the *kathakali* dance dramas) but as far south as Java and Bali is surely one of the lesser, but nonetheless most remarkable, spiritual wonders of the world.

THE BALINESE AT PLAY

SILVER RAIN

Old Balinese princes used to pay for the formation of large and splendid orchestras (*gamelan*) in which they then performed themselves, no doubt with considerable display of self-congratulation, rather as the princelings of eighteenth-century German courts would play the cello or the flute and elicit works with prominent, but not too difficult, parts for their instrument from Bach or Mozart.

This patronage by the jovial rajahs of old, dividing their time between *gamelan*-playing and the demands of their innumerable wives, has given way to support by the local community associations *(banjar)* and a competitive ambiance fostered by the training courses in *gamelan* music given by the colleges of higher education in Denpasar.

Though the *gamelan* derive historically from the indigenous orchestras of old Java, the music they play in Bali today is alto-

gether more lively and progressive than anything you'll hear on the larger island. Though it may seem at first that what you're hearing is a highly stylized and traditional art form, the truth is that new styles within that form are constantly being evolved, and Balinese *gamelan* music is very much a living and growing genre.

What characterizes the Balinese *gamelan* is its brilliance of sound, its sudden changes of volume and pace, and its virtuoso displays of very precise, very fast playing.

Two key features have to be understood. As with Balinese drama, the performers are not professional, and the music exists primarily as an accompaniment to rituals and dance performances (themselves also accompaniments to rituals) rather than as an entertainment in its own right. Of course, there are exceptions nowadays, such as the uprooted and rather sad-looking perform-

Balinese *gamelan* musicians. The music is almost entirely percussive in nature and has been described by one writer as "a shining rain of silver", by another as "the muffled laughter of forgotten gods".

ers seated in the lobbies of some big hotels playing with commendable spirit for a set portion of every hour. But the overwhelming majority of the musicians in Bali are farmers during the day, and very highly trained *gamelan* artists after sundown.

If you want to judge how genuine the *gamelan* you're seeing is, count the number of performers. A real *gamelan gong*, the commonest type of modern band, will have around twenty players and feature the following instruments:

Xylophone-like instruments known as *gangsa*. These consist of bronze keys over bamboo resonators that are beaten with a mallet held in the right hand and their reverberation immediately cut short by the thumb and index finger of the left.

A *riong*, a frame holding bronze "pots" which four players strike with sticks.

A *trompong*, an instrument similar to the above but played by a virtuoso solo player.

A *ceng ceng*, a frame with many cymbals suspended from it — these are struck by another, hand-held cymbal.

Kendang, drums. These are the heart of the *gamelan*, the only instruments the dancers need attend to and played by the seasoned maestros of the orchestra. The first drummer is like the first violinist and conductor of a Western classical orchestra combined, the leader and controller of the *gamelan*.

The musicians will all be male, will be seated on the ground and dressed in the brilliant uniform of their particular orchestra.

The instruments are of invariable pitch, fixed forever at the time of manufacture. Where instruments are paired, there is often a slight and deliberate difference between their respective pitches designed to set up a deliciously thrilling dissonance that is an essential component in the brilliant, metallic cascade of sound that is Balinese music.

Here, then, is a music that, unless extra instruments are added, is entirely percussive. Nothing could be further removed from the Western classical tradition where the timpani have the lowest status of all the instruments in the orchestra. In Bali, they are

Gamelan music and street processions often combine to add delight to the most oppressively humid day.

everything, and the result is a music that injects energy into the sultry night air, a music so vibrant and electrifying that the name *kebyar gamelan* says it all. *Kebyar* means bursting into flower, flaring up suddenly into jagged, passionate brilliance.

The American Colin McPhee, author of *A House in Bali* (see BIBLIOGRAPHY), can be credited with first bringing this unique music to the notice of the West. He must have known his own attempts to transcribe the music for two pianos were doomed from the start, but the influence persisted nonetheless, in America especially, and found its first major flowering on the international scene in the sixties with the music of such artists as Steve Reich, Terry Riley and, later, Philip Glass.

DANCE AND DRAMA

While only men play in the *gamelan* orchestras, the dance dramas are truly androgynous, with women and men dancing a wide variety of roles, sometimes as the opposite sex, sometimes as their own, and sometimes as animals. The style is essentially Javanese, and before that Indian, but with Balinese, spirit-ritual elements added.

Training is very intensive and begins young. Balinese dance has always made great use of children, and girls destined for the *legong* dance start at six or seven with training that includes special massage to make their limbs supple. Hand and head movements are especially important, leg movements — in total contrast to Western dance of all styles — less so. Facial expressions and the movement of the eyes are most important of all.

Despite the long training, dancers are not paid, at least not when performing traditional festival dances at the temples. The wide variety of dances in Bali is always being added to, old styles falling out of favor and new ones coming into fashion. In this, Balinese dance contrasts with the unaltering classical dance of Java from which it derives.

The difference comes from dance in Bali being a popular art form, rooted in collective social organizations, whereas in Java it was for centuries something performed under the patronage of the rajahs and nowadays is staged almost exclusively for tourists.

Balinese dances were originally, and are still generally, sacred, performed to greet the gods as they descend from their mountaintop homes into the temples to attend the temple ceremonies.

However, special abbreviated dance shows are now put on specifically for visitors. These take place either at the bigger hotels at Sanur or Nusa Dua or in villages such as Ubud, Batubulan or Bona.

There won't be any Balinese at these tourist shows, apart from the odd child selling soft drinks or "programs" who might stay on to watch. There will be raked seating provided so that everyone gets an uninterrupted view, there will be an attempt at modern theatrical lighting, and the shows will begin at a convenient time.

But what you will see will not be the dance drama, performed in the crowded forecourt of a temple attended by the entire village population dressed for a high festival, that made Bali famous in the thirties. Not only will any performance done as a routine for an audience the artists know have little if any knowledge of the art form inevitably lack fire; the whole context will be missing, and what you will be witnessing will be an art torn up from its roots and presented in a vacuum.

Nevertheless, there are of course different levels of artistry in these shows, and it should be said at once that the dances at **Ubud**, the large village north of Denpasar that is the "cultural capital" of Bali, are usually of a high quality and only the original social context is missing.

At Ubud, a different program is offered each night of the week, either at the Ubud Palace or elsewhere. Where the performances are outside the village itself, transport is provided and the cost included in the price of the ticket.

The *legong* performance, currently presented on Mondays at the Palace, is really a kind of revue. It features a number of different dances, with the *legong* itself some two-

---

All the sultry, languid beauty of the tropics is suggested by this young performer in the *barong* dance. Children are trained in the art of dance from an early age, and then often continue to perform throughout their adult lives.

thirds of the way through. The standard is very high and, despite the fact that this performance is put on exclusively for the benefit of foreigners, this is an excellent introduction to Balinese dance.

Danced against a background of the temple, the combination of the hard, precise music, the rich costumes, and the dedication on the faces of the young performers is very powerful. That the lighting is improvised, some of it consisting of domestic light-bulbs with biscuit-tin reflectors, only adds to the authenticity and excitement of the performance.

At **Bona**, half an hour's drive east of Denpasar, shows are given nightly at various sites. The village is not easily accessible by public transport after sunset and audiences are almost invariably brought in by the various tour agencies in Kuta and Sanur. The performance areas, lit by torches in preparation for the *kecak* dance, make a picturesque sight as you drive past them in the early Indonesian dark. The performances themselves, however, can be rather less impressive.

The standard fare at Bona is a *kecak* dance followed by two spirit possession dances, the *sanghyang dedari* and the *sanghyang jaran*. The convenience of this arrangement for the organizers is that none of these dances requires a *gamelan* accompaniment.

At **Batubulan**, north of Denpasar on the road to Gianyar, *barong* dances are performed, again exclusively for visitors, at 9 am every morning. The show lasts an hour.

Bali's Dances

The following are the main dances and other dramatic performances you are likely to encounter on the island.

Arja Sometimes referred to as "Balinese opera," this is really ballet and opera combined. Four women, playing male characters, sing and dance simultaneously. Clowns and servants provide the low-life commentary.

A gorgeously clad figure from the *kecak* dance approaches the flaming lamp that is this dance's only illumination. The dance has no instrumental accompaniment and is based on a story from the Indian *Ramayana* epic.

Baris Gede A warrior dance for a group of a dozen or so middle-aged men, its purpose is to protect the visiting gods at temple festivals from evil spirits. The dancers wear headdresses with a triangle of white cloth at the back, and with pieces of shell attached. They carry spears tipped with peacock feathers, and during the dance divide into two groups and engage in mock conflict.

Baris Pendet A solo form of the above. In this demanding virtuoso dance, the performer goes through all the emotions of a warrior before, and then in, battle.

Barong Essentially an exorcism dance, the *barong* features a benign monster — the *barong ket* — rather like the lion in the Chinese lion dance, but with long white hair and fitted with leather saddles. Its mouth opens and shuts noisily. Its opponent is the *rangda*, a witch with long white hair, drooping breasts, bulging eyes and twisted fangs, flourishing a magically powerful white cloth.

The full version begins with introductory dances unconnected to the main action — a comic confrontation between the *barong* and three masked palm-wine tappers, and a short *legong* dance.

The play proper's essential feature is a battle between the good-natured *barong* and the *rangda*, with the *barong* assisted, not very effectively, by a group of men armed with *kris* (short swords). What leads up to this is a plot involving a queen who has to sacrifice her son to the goddess of death. The son is saved, being given immortality by the god Siwa, but takes on a variety of heroic tasks which quickly prove too much for him. He calls on the *barong* for help, and the *barong* in turn calls on the armed warriors.

The *rangda* puts a spell on the men so that they try to kill themselves. The *barong*, however, renders their swords harmless, and the impotent frenzy of the entranced warriors is a big feature of the show.

The *rangda* is finally defeated, but real magic is considered to have been brought forth by the performance — and indeed the warriors are often in an actual trance by this

In the sword (*kris*) dance, usually seen as the culmination of a temple's *odalan* festival, entranced men attempt to wound themselves with sharpened weapons. They never succeed.

stage — and so a chicken is sacrificed and water sprinkled on the warriors by a resident *pemangku* as a conclusion to the dance.

Barong Landong The name means "tall barong," and this performance features two large figures, twice life size, manipulated by actors inside them. They enact a comic slanging-match between a black giant, *jero gede*, and his woman, *jero luh*. The little chanted drama is accompanied by a few musicians and is in reality a rite to dispel evil performed on important occasions such as the night before a cremation.

Calon Arang An exorcism drama aimed at the local village witches *(leyak* — see MAGIC AND WITCHCRAFT, page 49) and usually performed when a new temple is dedicated.

Staged at the full moon, and continuing until dawn, the drama features the witch *rangda* who, at the climax of the performance, after comic interludes and dances by young girls, emerges from her house and advances in a frenzy on the audience.

The part of the *rangda* is taken by an experienced older actor because the performance involves the witch going into an entranced rage, possessed — so the Balinese believe — by the spirit of the actual *rangda*. The end of the event is unpredictable, and the *rangda* can on occasion run amok. Only an actor of long experience can hope to control so powerful a spirit entering into him.

The purpose of the performance is to placate the *rangda* by demonstrating her power, and thus gain her cooperation against the lesser witches in the village.

The performance raises many profound questions, such as the extent to which any acting anywhere is a form of self-imposed possession, and the reasons for the world-wide obsession with solitary women past the age of childbearing as agents of evil (*rangda* means widow).

Gambuh An ancient Balinese dance performed to entertain visiting gods at temple festivals.

Speaking in Kawi, a prince and his beloved undergo various trials to the accompaniment of an antique orchestra featuring bass flutes. Comic servants provide a commentary in Low Balinese.

Janger Twelve girls and twelve boys sit on four sides of a square with a leader in the middle. They perform a variety of dances, comic sketches and acrobatic displays.

Jauk A short dance by a masked dancer displaying the sinister convolutions of a demon.

Joged A non-temple dance that was much appreciated by early visitors to the island anxious to penetrate the ceremonious reserve of the Balinese. A solo girl dances flirtatiously with men she selects from the audience. Sometimes it is performed by a boy dressed as a woman, in which case it's called *gandrung*.

Kebiyar Duduk The Balinese emphasis on eyes, head and arms in dance, as opposed to legs, is highlighted in this dance for a solo seated performer. It's essentially an abstract interpretation of Balinese music and was invented in the thirties by the famous Balinese dancer known as Mario — his career is described by Covarrubias in *The Island of Bali* (see BIBLIOGRAPHY).

Kecak There is no accompanying orchestra in this dance. Instead, a large group of men provides a continuous vocal background, something like a sound-picture of

OPPOSITE: The sword (*kris*) dance demonstrated at a show for tourist. ABOVE: The evil *rangda* from the *barong* dance. Dance is arguably the finest flower of Balinese art.

an ocean in all its moods. They are dressed only in a black and white check sarong, with a red flower behind the right ear and a white one behind the left.

They move around on their haunches, sometimes swaying from this side to that, sometimes bouncing up and down, sometimes flinging themselves forward in a circle, with arms outstretched toward the center.

All the time they chant, sometimes in unison, sometimes contrapuntally, between sections of the group.

The central performance area is lit only by a flaming lamp, but the gorgeously clad characters in the drama to which the group of men provide an accompaniment usually arrive on the scene through a temple gateway, dramatically lit from behind.

The story is of Rama's trip to the forest with Sita to seek the golden deer. Rawana, king of the demons, kidnaps Sita, but Hanuman, the white monkey, comes to her aid by telling Rama what's happened. A son of the demon king fires an arrow (that turns into a snake) at Rama, but Rama calls on Garuda, the bird god, to save him. The king of the monkeys, Sugriwa, then arrives on the scene and the drama ends with a fight between the monkeys and the demons, with the *kecak* chorus dividing in support of the two sides. Rama is reunited with his beloved Sita.

ABOVE: *Kecak* Dance. OPPOSITE: Seated dancer — arms and eyes are far more important in Balinese dance than the legs, and this makes it far removed from every kind of Western dance. It is, of course, Indian in origin.

Kupu Kupu Carum A dance in which a prince manages through meditation to overcome the temptations offered him by a band of nymphs. The actor playing the prince remains motionless throughout most of the performance.

Legong This most classical of all Balinese dances used only to be performed by girls who had not yet reached puberty. It is performed by three dancers, two of them enacting the principal characters and the third playing the *condong* or servant.

The dance is so formalized, with the dancers portraying first one incident then another without any change of style, that it is very difficult to follow what's going on. But, for the record, the plot involves a princess, Rangkesari, who has been forcibly abducted by a prince, Lasem. She refuses to have anything to do with him, and when she hears her brother, the crown prince of Kahuripan, is coming to save her, she appeals to her captor to release her and so avoid a battle. He refuses, and on his way out to fight sees a raven, an omen of his imminent defeat on the battlefield.

The dance tells only a fragment of this brief story. It begins with the condong dancing a prologue, then shows the two identically dressed girls as the prince and princess. The prince is already about to leave for the battlefield when they first appear. He is sad that the princess has rejected him; she asks him not to fight her brother; he refuses and leaves. The *condong* then closes the performance by appearing with little gilt wings attached, representing the bird of ill omen.

Such highly stylized dramatic forms, showing only the climax of a story already well known to the audience, and even that symbolically and without any actual confrontation, has characterized highly developed forms of theater elsewhere, in ancient Greece and in Japan, for example. Here in Bali, the *legong* has a particularly remote quality given to it by its being played by (originally) very young girls dressed in exceptionally elaborate costumes.

There is no mention of the *legong* in the ancient *lontar* (palm-leaf books) referring to dance, and the form was probably created as recently as the nineteenth century.

Mendet (also known as *Pendet*) A dance to welcome the spirits to the temple performed by a group of older women carrying offerings in their right hands.

Oleg Tambulilingan A dance representing the flirtation between two bees gathering honey among the flowers.

Panyembrama A welcoming dance performed by a troupe of girls who scatter flowers on the spectators. It was evolved in the sixties as an introductory dance for the "legong revue" performances.

Prembon A masked dance showing the defeat by Sri Krisna Kapakisan of rebellious subjects using a magical sword given him by Gaja Mada.

Ramayana Ballet Imported to Bali recently from Java, this dance tells the story of Rama and Hanuman (the white monkey) from the *Ramayana* epic. It's the same story told in the *kecak* dance.

Rejang A stately, processional movement performed by women bringing offerings to a temple.

Sanghyang Dedari (also called the Virgin Dance) A possession dance in which two young girl dancers are put into a trance. The only music is chanting by unaccompanied voices.

Sanghyang Jaran (also called the Fire Dance) This is an event rather than a dance, in which a young man enters riding a hobbyhorse and proceeds to trample with his bare feet on a pile of smoldering coconut husks. The performer is in a trance and sometimes kicks the glowing shells around quite violently. They're raked back into a heap by an assistant. Afterwards, the entranced youth is brought back to normal consciousness with water. He then drinks holy water three times and offers blossoms three times in the direction of the temple.

Topeng Pajegan A masked dance in which a solo dancer performs in a series of different masks to portray a variety of characters in a story.

Topeng Panca A masked dance in which a number of dancers, each wearing a different mask, act out a story.

Topeng Tua A solo masked dance, slow and deliberate, in which the dancer imitates the uncertain and painful movements of a very old man.

Wayang Wong A rare form of drama where actors enact the stories from the shadow puppet plays.

You can attend dance classes, held in the mornings, at two colleges in the capital — see DENPASAR section for details.

A six-week Bali Arts Festival is held in Denpasar from mid-June to the end of July every year featuring a good deal of music and dance.

Finally, the Badung Government Tourist Office on Jalan Surapati in Denpasar (☏ 23399 and 23602) issues an up-to-date broadsheet with details of imminent temple festivals, many of which will include dance performances.

SHADOWS IN THE DARK

The shadow-puppet play (*wayang* — puppet, *kulit* — leather) you are most likely to see will have been staged specifically for tourists. But there are at least a couple of dozen practicing puppeteers in Bali staging performances on request for weddings, temple anniversaries and the night before cremations.

The *wayang kulit* is, like almost all art in Bali, ceremonial in origin, and the puppeteer *(dalang)* a kind of magician.

The artist as seer is an old idea, and it's no surprise that the Indonesian puppet play — it's also found in Java — is seen by many as a form of metaphysics. Sukarno, the country's first president, used to gather his ministers together in his hill-station retreat and tease them with puppet shows which they didn't have to look very far to see prefigured their advancement or fall from grace. Even now there are commentators who attribute the blank passivity of the people in the face of the massacre of leftists in 1965 to a fatalism rooted in the mythology of the *wayang*, a belief that, in the eternal battle between good and evil, there was no hope for you if, in the episode of the drama which happened to constitute

The *wayang kulit*, or shadow-puppet play. The *dalang*, or puppeteer, sits behind his screen and selects his puppets from a collection in a large wooden box. The stories are well-known to the local audience in advance — they have to be as only the jokes are in a language the ordinary people understand.

your life, you were unfortunate enough to be caught on the wrong side of the stage.

The "stage" in the *wayang* is a cloth screen some one meter by three. The right as you, the audience, view it is the side of the bug-eyed villains, the left of the strangely emaciated aristocratic heroes.

On a low platform behind the screen sits the *dalang*, cross-legged and formally dressed as if for a religious ceremony, which in a way this is. To his left is the puppet box containing a large selection of the puppets in regular use. Behind him, dressed in sa-

rong and headdress, sit the musicians of the *gender wayang* behind their *gangsa*, the xylophone-like instruments of the *gamelan*. No gongs or drums are used, and the *gangsa* are struck by hammers held in each hand. Consequently the reverberation has to be stopped by the knuckles rather than the left hand as in the *gamelan* proper.

The performance begins with an overture by the musicians during which the puppeteer sprinkles holy water and makes offerings to sanctify the show and "bring the puppets to life." The show itself begins with a kind of skeletal leaf (but actually the sacred Tree of Life) dividing the screen. It will be used again later to indicate changes of scene.

The stories are all taken from the *Ramayana* and *Mahabharata* epics (see HEROES AND VILLAINS, p. 50) and are well known in advance to the Balinese, just as the story of Cinderella will be known in advance to Western audiences at a pantomime, or *Don Giovanni* to the opera-goer. The attraction of the performance is both the telling-over of an old tale and the up-to-date and local references the *dalang* will manage somehow or other to incorporate into it.

It's as well the stories are known already because the actual narration will be chanted in the dead Javanese language of Kawi, and the language of the ordinary people will only appear in the sarcastic and debunking remarks of the four low-life "clowns".

Thus at every *wayang* play not only does society witness a highlighting and a confirmation of the established social order, it also is made conscious of the interplay of this world with that of the gods, and in a way that makes life seem just a part of a greater enactment over which it's foolish to think we have any measure of control.

It's important to realize you have every right to go backstage and watch the show from the other side. There'll even be a couple of benches provided, one on each side of the performers. And it's here, behind the scenes, that the real atmosphere of the *wayang* can best be flavored.

It's an enclosed, primordial scene. The flaming lamp, clearly visible even from front-of-house and giving the flickering effect of early film to the show as a whole, is seen backstage as being a giant kettle with flames leaping from its stubby, wick-crammed spout.

The puppets themselves, you'll see, are intricately shaped, and painted in great detail, with much gilt — quite unnecessarily for their function as casters of shadows, but very appropriately for sacral adjuncts. A string, worked by the *dalang*'s index finger, moves the puppet's jaw, while a thin stick, manipulated with the puppeteer's other hand, operates the arm of any character that appears solo.

An assistant sits on either side of the puppeteer and prepares and then hands him the puppets as he needs them from a banana tree trunk into which they've been stuck ready for use. The puppets' traveling box stands away to the puppeteer's left and, sitting cross-legged, he beats on the box with a peg held between the toes of his right foot, providing rhythmic excitement and special effects for the innumerable fights into which the stories always, and rather quickly, descend.

The puppeteer does all the talking, telling the story and acting all the speaking parts. Sweat running down his face from the hot night and the heat of the lamp, he pours out a stream of jokes, chants and heroic invocations, beating the screen with his flimsy

facing this way and then that, and each change accompanied by a clack with the toe-hammer. The old tackle, the flaring light, the relish of the exuberant puppeteer... it's akin to the Sicilian puppets of Palermo re-enacting stories of the crusades based on the rhyming epics of Ariosto or Tasso. It has the same enclosed quality, the same intensity.

Here in the tropics it's older still. What you're seeing is something so old that scholars are unable to ascribe a place of origin to it. Yet here it is being re-created yet again in

puppets and simultaneously hammering the box with his foot.

The guttering flame is replenished by the "evil-side" (puppeteer's left) attendant pouring oil into the lidless kettle. A shield behind concentrates the light onto the screen and keeps it out of the eyes of the puppeteer. The costumed musicians hammer away, interweaving their arpeggios and changing rhythm for every new scene and facet of the immemorially ancient story.

It's an extraordinary scene, these stories from far-off India being reenacted in the tropical night and with such a combination of relish and formality. The eager, laughing faces of the audience, the constant reversing of the puppets, so that they appear first

this wall-less village hall, by the sweating, laughing but be-hatted puppeteer.

It's the magic of the old Javanese night. And the puppeteer, as well as actually being a priest, is also a magician, able to bring to life these ancient stories with his two-dimensional dolls. He stirs the naturally symbolic imaginations of the people, warming their easily warmed hearts with his gusto and his mixture of heroism and broad popular comedy.

The *wayang kulit*. OPPOSITE: The puppeteer, both magician and priest, both jester and guardian of an extraordinarily ancient tradition. ABOVE: The primordial scene backstage — you're welcome to go round and take a look. On the whole it's more exciting that out front.

The popularity of these old night entertainments shows how deep they go into the consciousness of the people. These flickering images in jungle villages beside elaborately wrought Hindu temples have for centuries molded the souls of a naturally artistic people with stories of magic, power struggles, good and evil, and seemingly pointless heroism.

When in 1909 the Balinese aristocracy presented themselves before the Dutch army for certain destruction in long lines of bejeweled and costumed splendor, the images and pat-

terns of the heroic tales of the *wayang kulit* cannot have been far from their hearts. Like the Pandavas and the Kouravas at war in the *Mahabharata*, they could never surrender.

THE AFFRIGHTED SUN

The gamecock clipped and armed for fight
Does the rising sun affright.
— William Blake, *Auguries of Innocence* (1805)

ABOVE: A fighting cook and its master.
OPPOSITE: Men preening and matching their fighting cocks — a common sight all over Bali. Cock fights are nowadays only permitted before temple anniversary ceremonies as a precaution against excessive gambling.

The tending and care of fighting cocks is one of the most visible parts of Balinese life, and men sitting in circles preening their birds is one of the commonest sights on the island.

All gambling has been illegal throughout Indonesia since 1981. In Bali, however, where the letting of blood is deemed a necessary part of temple festivals, permits are issued by the police allowing three cockfights on the days of temple anniversary celebrations. Both the restriction on the number of fights and the general prohibition on gambling are regularly ignored on these occasions.

Bets are placed nominally in the ancient currency of the ringgit though in reality in the rupiah equivalent. A lay priest (*pemangku*) gives offerings to both the good and evil spirits before the fight begins.

The Balinese for cockfights is *tajen* (blades), the razor-sharp knives that are attached to the cocks' left legs.

Cocks naturally fight each other over the female birds, and this is what they do in the trial bouts you can see on any sunny afternoon. But it's only with these lethal blades attached that they slash their opponent almost to death, often in a matter of seconds. They don't experience the blades in the trial bouts, of course. Then suddenly, in the fight itself, nature becomes hideously armed, a flurry in the air becomes a flashing of steel, with the defeated bird lying bleeding in the dust.

This isn't the end. The blade becomes the property of the specialist (*pekembar*) the owner has employed to fix it in place. As soon as the winner has been declared, the legs, the blade attached, are chopped off the losing cock, almost invariably while it is still alive.

To deplore this casual cruelty may be judged a Western prejudice inappropriate to Asia, but the pain is real enough for the cock wherever it happens. I have seen Balinese cocks lying exhausted and wounded, suffering the humiliation of defeat and the agony of laceration, start up from the earth at what is clearly the most horrific pain imaginable. And this is the eventual fate reserved for every one of the creatures so lovingly caressed by their doting owners of former days.

CRICKET-FIGHTING

The Balinese also bet on crickets; it's a sort of poor-man's cockfighting. The creatures are caught in the cracks of the dried-out rice fields after harvest and fed on grains of rice and flower petals. They are exercised and bathed, and kept in tubular cages made of sections of bamboo. The fights take place inside a pair of cages placed together end to end. The winner is the cricket that forces the other to retreat to its furthest corner. Bets are

accompany the gods on their way down to the temples. Whatever their original purpose, the unexpected sound of these tiny instruments borne on the breeze is one of the real delights of the island.

ARTS AND CRAFTS

PAINTING

Some people go to Bali to buy paintings. Balinese art acquired some celebrity before

in the region of a few thousand rupiah — on cocks they can be millions.

BIRD ORCHESTRAS

Bells and small flutes are attached round the necks of doves so that when they wheel overhead they produce a delicious tinkling and humming. Covarrubias says in *The Island of Bali* (see BIBLIOGRAPHY) that these aerial musical instruments are a protection against birds of prey. And it is true that if this is not the case, then bird orchestras are the only form of Balinese music created purely for pleasure.

Even so, it would be very Balinese to make them for fun, and then say they were to

the war due to the publicity given it by artists from the West coming to live on the island. They found a prolific but static local tradition, and encouraged the practitioners to experiment on semi-Western lines. The results proved exotic yet familiar, just the thing the well-heeled tourists needed to take home as mementos. But the truth is, things aren't what they were.

It may well be true that you can resell Balinese pictures in the Gulf States and else-

OPPOSITE and ABOVE: The terrors that await evil-doers in the afterlife, and the glee with which their tormentors go about their work, are vividly depicted on the walls of the Kertha Gosa (the ancient Court House) in Klungkung. The pictures are modern copies of older originals.

where for a handsome profit, if you know where to take them. But the fact remains there is a vast amount of junk being produced merely to satisfy the most elementary preconceptions as to what a painting by a Balinese artist might be like.

Much of the worst can be bypassed by going direct to Ubud, the center for Balinese painting both good and mediocre. Here at least you will have a chance to inspect a wide range of work — particularly conveniently at the gallery set apart across a rice field to the left of the Puri Lukisan Museum where paintings by many artists hang with

prices (not necessarily final) attached. A visit here will allow you to compare styles and going rates before you begin looking at the galleries showing only the owner's work.

Balinese painting before the thirties was exclusively concerned with the production of hangings and calendars for temples. Production was centered on Kamasan, south of Klungkung, and work of this kind is now referred to as being in the Kamasan style. Subjects were scenes from the epic stories, painted in hand-ground paints, and the final result was not unlike a colored version of the *wayang kulit* shadow puppet plays. These kind of paintings are still available, and still being produced, in Kamasan itself.

ABOVE: A Balinese painting from a private collection. The rural scene, and the crowding of the canvas with largely decorative detail, is very typical of the so-called "traditional" school of painting.

from Campuhan. Their pictures are vividly colored naive versions of daily-life scenes.

Of course there are some fine pictures among all these, though originality is not a strong suit in the Balinese hand. But prices are not low, whatever the quality — you will have to start thinking in terms of at least US$200 as an absolute minimum for a small-sized production if you want to acquire anything at all reasonable.

The booklet *Different Styles of Painting in Bali* by Drs Sudarmaji, available at the Neka Gallery in Ubud (not to be confused with the Museum Neka) is helpful in getting an idea of what to expect.

WOOD-CARVING

Balinese wood-carving is renowned because a natural local aptitude has allowed itself to be influenced by sophisticated Western styles, and the resulting hybrid artifacts consequently differ from anything found anywhere else. The main place to see wood-carvings in Bali is the village of Mas, south of Ubud.

The craftsmen of earlier times were occupied with carving figures of gods and heroes for the adornment of the palaces of the local rajahs. The depiction of animals and trees, as well as non-traditional fantasy figures, came with the arrival of Western artists. A particular style involving smooth surfaces and elongated human bodies has become common, and is often looked on as quintessentially Balinese, but actually is only something evolved in the thirties in imitation of the European Art Nouveau style.

As with all art objects, the only advice that can be given is to buy only what you yourself consider to be of high quality. Despite the endless duplication, there are some wonderful craftsmen at work. Fashioning the wood with delicate steel tools and a lightweight hammer, and working with extraordinary speed, they have gained the reputation of being among of the finest wood-carvers anywhere in the world.

Painted carvings, made from local soft woods, are cheap and produced in huge numbers. Imitation fruit — bananas in par-

For the rest, styles are nowadays divided into "traditional" and "young artists." By traditional is meant the style of painting encouraged in the thirties by the Western artists Rudolf Bonnet and Walter Spies, painters who settled in Bali and lived in Campuhan, down by Ubud's suspension bridge. These pictures depict daily scenes as well as legendary ones, in restrained colors or even monochrome. They are comparatively realistic, though filling every corner of the canvas with detail, and lacking any real attempt at light and shade effects.

The so-called young artists were set to work by the Dutch painter Arie Smit in the sixties and are based in Penestanan, an extension of Ubud just over the bridge ticular — are almost all produced in the village of Pujung (see THE BROAD HIGHWAY, page 136), yet can be found on sale all over the world.

Hardwood carvings are generally produced using imported wood as Bali's climate does not give rise to classic equatorial rain forests. Ebony, for instance, is imported from Kalimantan and Sulawesi in eastern Indonesia.

Beware of imitations of these woods. If you want to be sure your ebony is ebony, there's one sure-fire test: ebony doesn't float. Whether your retailer will allow you to test it is, of course, another matter.

The famous shop for wood-carvings in Mas is Ida Bagus Tilem's. This is where presidents and millionaires buy their Bali souvenirs. Quality is guaranteed, but prices are very high: a place, perhaps, to see the best, then seek out comparable specimens in the numerous smaller establishments elsewhere in the village.

THE OTHER FACE

Masks (*topeng*) are an important element in Balinese dance, and foreigners have been quick to see them as eminently desirable items.

Every actor knows the power of a mask. Hanging on a wall, it's just decorative. Put it on and, in an extraordinary way, it becomes alive, a part of you — but of a different you, an altogether new you. The mask and you combine to become something neither of you was before.

The Balinese are quick to interpret this psychological phenomenon as a sacred power that inhabits the mask. Many masks represent gods, and as the head is considered the most sacred part of the body, the special status of masks in Bali is assured.

Masks are mostly made at Mas and Singapadu out of the wood of the *pule*, the tree called in Australia the milky pine.

Balinese temple stone-carvings — a sense of humor is frequently on show, while some happily display eroticism in the Hindu tradition. Stone-carving is one of the cheaper art forms to acquire, and almost all Balinese homes display some examples.

TAKE-AWAY SHRINES

Carved stone is everywhere in Bali. Boss-eyed monsters with lolling tongues and long fangs cohabit happily with figures on flowery motorbikes, and there are not only no temples but few public buildings or private houses that don't boast at least some examples of the art.

Stone-carving is unlike wood-carving in that Western stylistic influence has been minimal, though figures from nature, as opposed to mythology, have long been incorporated into the designs. And Balinese wit, with wry comments on modern fashions, is everywhere.

Stone-carvings also differ from wood-carvings in that the ordinary Balinese can afford to buy them. Prices are often very low, as little as Rp5,000 for the smallest pieces. The only problem for the visitor is weight — even so, little items a few centimeters high are on sale, and of just about any animal, bird, mythological or fanciful character you could wish for.

Almost all Balinese stone-carving goes on at Batubulan, home of the tourist version of the *barong* dance and on the road from Denpasar to Gianyar. Shops and workshops are one and the same, and all prices are negotiable.

The stone carved is a very soft sandstone, extremely easy to work but very friable. So pack your purchases carefully when taking them home, and remember they'll weather fast if kept outdoors. To some people, though, the temptation to have a mock-Balinese shrine in the garden may be irresistible.

ENDEK, *IKAT* AND BATIK

Weaving enthusiasts will be eager to seek out the local handmade cloth, *endek*, where a pattern has been dyed into the weft by tying it here and there with strips of plastic. The cloth is made on old European-style handlooms in small factories, and is sold for local consumption in markets all over Bali.

Ikat, a cloth for which *both* warp and weft have been prepattern-dyed, is pro-

duced and sold in the Bali Aga village of Tenganan. It's an appallingly complex and time-consuming procedure, and you naturally pay for this when you buy the finished product.

Most visitors, however, will be content with the better-known batik from Java. Batik is not a Balinese product (though "Bali patterns" are always on offer) but both the brilliant "new" and the more delicately shaded "old" batik are on sale in all the main towns, and more or less everywhere that tourists frequent.

All three cloths are sold either direct from the bolt or made up into attractive, if not always very modern, articles of clothing.

GOLD AND SILVER

Despite the claims on the front of shops in Celuk, the center for gold in Bali is a small area of Denpasar, at the junction of Jalan Sulawesi and Jalan Hasanudin. Here, items of jewelry are sold by weight, prices follow the current price of gold, and the shops cater

---

Balinese silverware — the subjects are usually sacred and the technique invariably superb. The center for silverware is the village of Celuk.

primarily to rich Balinese rather than to visitors and foreign tourists.

Celuk, just past Batubulan coming out from Denpasar on the way to Gianyar or Ubud, is the silverware center. Intricately worked items — anything from rings to tableware — are a specialty, the smaller pieces virtually solid silver, the larger ones silver-plated. You can watch the silversmiths at work, and prices are very reasonable.

RIJSTTAFFEL **TO** *KRETEK*

FESTIVE FOODS

Humans, like animals, are astonishingly conservative where food is concerned. It seems that we learn to like what we are fed in childhood, modify this slightly by adventures in early adult life, and then stick to the limited repertoire we have acquired to the end of our days.

Consequently, Balinese food, being very different from what Westerners are used to, is unlikely to appeal to the average visitor anxious for the consolations of what he knows when he sits down to dinner after having been faced elsewhere with so much that was strange.

Besides, the local fare on ordinary days is very basic. Normal food for the Balinese is cold boiled or steamed rice *(nasi)* with a side dish of chopped and very highly spiced vegetables. This is prepared early in the day and left out, covered with squares of banana leaf, for members of the household to help themselves to whenever they feel hungry. It's eaten, with the right hand and preferably alone, on a banana-leaf plate that is then thrown to the pigs.

At festivals, however, far more complex dishes are prepared, and these, together with the tasty bits and pieces the Balinese love to eat at street stalls, are what the visitor is most likely to come across in the hotels and local restaurants. Only in the villages, or in the smaller eating places such as in Kuta's Night Market (see page 119), will you encounter the real thing.

Satay is popular all over Indonesia. Here the tiny kebabs are waiting to be grilled on a street-side stall. They're usually eaten with a spicy peanut sauce.

Among these festive dishes, the best known is *be guling*, roast pork. It'll be marketed for you as *babi guling*, and you'll be told this means Balinese roast suckling pig. But the animal you'll be eating will have been three to six months old, barely a suckling, and *babi* is anyway Indonesian, not Balinese. *Be* means meat and *guling* turned.

Next is *bebek betutu*, roast duck, the least difficult to come to terms with of the Balinese festival foods.

Thirdly, *lawar*, or *ebat*, is a mixture of raw, finely chopped meat (usually turtle or pig) and fruits and spices, endlessly grated down.

Of the humbler local dishes, *nasi goreng* (fried rice) is the commonest, and what most visitors, uncertain of what other options might imply, tend to fall back on. It can be anything from sumptuous to little more than greasy rice with the odd shrimp, egg and spring onion mixed in.

Nasi campur is another cheap filler, steamed rice with bits and pieces of everything on top. *Gado gedo* is steamed bean-sprouts and vegetables, all under a sticky peanut sauce.

By contrast, the *rijsttaffel* was the Dutch colonial standby — a wide variety of different side-dishes served separately with steamed rice. It's usually ordered by a group, everyone taking what appeals to him.

Nasi padang is also a set of side dishes with rice, but it's true Indonesian (from the region of Padang in Sumatra), you can order only the things you fancy from a wide choice on the counter, and they all come highly spiced but cold.

Satay is a very popular Indonesian specialty, tiny kebabs — you usually order half a dozen or more — served with peanut or hot pepper sauce.

It won't be long before, having mastered some basic terms, you can begin to combine them, and recognize the combinations on menus. Thus, once you know chicken is *ayam*, coconut sauce *opor*, noodles *mee*, and bananas *pisang*, you won't have any problems identifying *ayam goreng* as fried chicken, *opor ayam* as chicken cooked in coconut sauce, *mee goreng* as fried noo-

dles and *pisang goreng* as banana fritters. Rice cakes, the usual Balinese breakfast, are *jaja*.

On offer with virtually everything is *kecap*, not ketchup (though the pronunciation is identical) but soy sauce; *manis* is sweet, *asin* salty.

In the resort areas of Bali, Western food is as common as or commoner than Indonesian. Menus are self-explanatory — though perhaps non-Australians will need to be told that jaffles are toasted sandwiches sealed at the edges so that the contents come molten and gently bubbling.

DRINKS

Cold drinks assume a new and vital significance in the Balinese climate. Supreme among these must be the exquisite mixtures made everywhere, but specially delicious on beaches, of fresh fruit, ice, syrup and a dash of canned milk whisked together in a blender. They're called simply *es jus*, iced juice, and the going rate on Kuta Beach is Rp500 (Rp700 if they're brought to you where you're lying on the sand). You can choose any combination of the listed fruits, or else tell them to put in something of everything. These gorgeous drinks seem to be Bali. The silky property given them by a high proportion of avocado or papaya takes them within range of paradise itself.

Everything else is in a lower class, though the flavored yoghurt drink, *lassi*, isn't far behind.

For the rest, *air jeruk* is lemon (or orange) juice, made with fresh fruit, while *stroop* is fruit cordial.

Much has been written about the danger of taking ice in the tropics. The cogent argument is that if the water the ice was made from wasn't boiled, the ice will contain any infection that was present in the water. True, and a point worth remembering in many places. But for some years now the ice in Bali has been produced in approved factories and is, if not one hundred per cent safe, widely accepted.

Vividly colored rice-cakes, *jaja*, the most popular breakfast with the Balinese.

Ordinary tap water is NOT drinkable.

Commercially produced ice cream is completely safe, but avoid the home-made variety peddled from street carts. Anything containing milk products needs careful handling and constant refrigeration in the tropics.

When it comes to alcohol, you are faced with the choice of rather expensive bottled products, similar to things you'll already know, and the very inexpensive local brews.

The latter are essentially three — *brem*, a very sweet wine made from black rice;

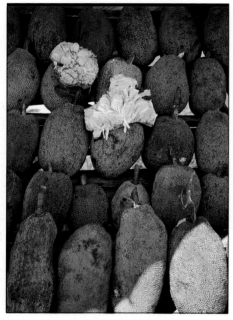

tuak, a form of sweetish beer made from the sugar of the coconut palm; and *arak*, a deceptively tasteless brandy distilled from either *tuak* or *brem*. *Arak* and *brem* mixed is excellent.

As for non-Balinese intoxicants, imported wine is usually very dear and consequently not much drunk, spirits are available but dropped in favor of *arak* by many visitors, while beer comes in three brands, Bintang, San Miguel and Anker, all more or less excellent.

Bali's fruits can be pleasures you never knew you liked until you tried them, like *salak* OPPOSITE and many other delights such as jackfruit ABOVE, mangosteen, durian, custard apples and mangoes.

For the rest, tea is *teh* and coffee *kopi*. Each can be taken with milk (*susu*), and will come ready-sweetened unless you specifically request it without sugar, in which case add the word *tawar*. Thus, coffee with milk but no sugar is *kopi susu tawar*.

TROPICAL FRUITS

The range of fruit available in Bali is almost a reason for going there in itself. Pineapples, papayas, coconuts, bananas, avocados — all are common and cheap. In addition there are a number of fruits you might be encountering for the first time — don't let this be a reason for not giving them a try. You don't want to find yourself tasting them for the first time on your last day and discovering, too late, that you were made for each other.

The following are the main attractions:

Salak — with a texture not unlike a Brazil nut but tasting like a lychee.

Rambutan — very like a lychee but with a hairy red skin.

Mangosteen — a fruit that travels badly and so is little known outside the tropics. The outside is black, brown or purple, and the inside stunning.

Blimbing — you can eat all of this refreshing pale green or yellow fruit. When cut, its cross-section is a five-pointed star, hence its Anglo-Saxon name star fruit.

Jambu-sotong — guavas.

Markisah — passion fruit. You'll see them on sale in the mountains — you break them open and eat everything you find inside, seeds and all. Exquisite is the only word for them.

Nangka — jackfruit. So big you'll only want to buy a segment. You eat the yellow inner part and discard the white outer layer.

Jeruk — the word refers to all citrus fruits, but the pomelo, or *jeruk bali*, is the commonest. It's like a grapefruit but bigger, and the taste is a lot sweeter. Lemons are *jeruk nipis*, ordinary oranges *jeruk manis*.

Durian — love it or loathe it, this is the infamous fruit that stinks, but tastes to some people like heaven. You can even get durian-flavored icecream — a good means of

judging whether or not you want to brave the real thing.

There are many more. If you see them on sale, give them a try. If you're worried you don't know which part to eat, ask the tradesman — street sellers in Indonesia will normally do just about anything to encourage you to buy. Just ask him to open one up for you, and if you don't trust his standard of hygiene, buy a couple and give him one, then eat them in tandem.

COCONUT PALMS

The Balinese venerate the coconut. The tree is such a generous provider, and considered such a friend to man, that, when I asked one hotel worker whether people were ever killed by coconuts falling to the ground, he said the tree was so kind he was quite sure it would never happen.

The coconut palm provides oil for cooking and lamps, sweet water to drink, flesh to eat or to make "milk" from for use in cooking, wood for house building and furniture, leaves for offerings, the "palm cabbage" (just below the head) for food, and gum from its flower buds for palm beer (*tuak*). Copra, the dried meat of the nut from which oil can easily be extracted, has been one of the main exports from the tropical belt for over a century.

SALT IN THE WOUND

An insight into the realities of the Third World life among which the tourist will find himself is provided by the economics of the salt-making business.

Salt in Bali is made from seawater, a process involving the carrying of large amounts of water from the sea onto the sand, carrying the wet sand into vats, the water from the vats into troughs and the final sludge from

The Balinese, too, sometimes find time to enjoy the beach. Their snacks, though very cheap, are an acquired taste. Note the fully-clad bathers. The Balinese have no tradition of sea-going, and until recent years the ordinary people tended to be afraid of the sea.

the troughs into filtering baskets. It's a family business, and an average family will produce 25 kg of salt a day during the dry season. The day's salt, product of at least two adults' labor, is sold for a grand total that averages out at Rp950 — about US$0.60. During the rainy season they produce nothing at all.

BETEL

Often, in the Balinese countryside, you'll come across what seems at first a terrifying spectacle — an older woman with lips stained scarlet, black teeth, a bulge in one cheek, and dribbling what looks like blood.

This is merely someone indulging in the very ancient and widespread Asian habit of chewing betel.

It's actually a combination of three basic ingredients folded together inside a betel leaf. Together they form a mild stimulant, aid to digestion and antiseptic all in one. But what is extraordinary, though hardly surprising, is that the Balinese have made it into a symbol of the three persons of God — Brahma, Wisnu and Siwa — and it is inconceivable for any temple offering to be made that doesn't include at least one sample.

JAMU

Jamu is a quintessentially Indonesian product, a herbal medicine marketed by a wide range of outlets, from teenage girls with ready-mixed concoctions on their backs doing the rounds in the early mornings to giant wholesalers and distributors of their patent, albeit traditional, medicines. Air Mancur is not an Indonesian domestic airline but the biggest name in this huge jamu trade.

The science of jamu originated from the central Javanese city of Solo, and virtually everyone connected with the industry is still Solonese.

Jamu's most celebrated claim is that it increases sexual potency. If you're interested in putting this claim to the test, and are not sure whether your Indonesian is up to explaining what you want in the local supermarket, try the itinerant vendors. They'll

probably be round far too early for you even to catch sight of them, but everyone else in Bali is up around 4 am and your room boy will undoubtedly be able to procure you a foul-tasting glassful. It will cost you around Rp300 — US$0.18. At that price, it's probably worth a try.

KRETEK

The first scent the arriving visitor receives on walking from his plane over to Immigration at Denpasar Airport is of cloves. This is altogether appropriate for what were once known as the Spice Islands, but the reason for the aroma today is that chopped cloves constitute 50 percent of Indonesia's most popular type of cigarette, kretek.

They're big business, and not least for the Indonesian government. The great Eiseman (see BIBLIOGRAPHY), admittedly using rather old statistics, estimates income from the tobacco industry constitutes 80 percent of all the country's tax revenue. He further reveals that, in one of the biggest tobacco companies' largest factories, every kretek cigarette is —believe it or not — rolled by hand.

OPPOSITE: The powers unleashed by even a judicious dose of the immensely popular jamu are not to be underestimated. In a culture that places great store on virility, aids to manliness are understandably in demand.

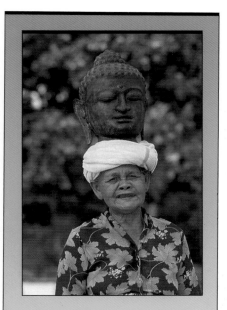

The
Broad
Highway

WITH its high mountains and low-lying coastal plains, Bali divides itself naturally into surprisingly self-defining areas. Not all, however, are of equal interest to the visitor. We have consequently dealt with those districts of most historical or contemporary interest at some length, and considered West Bali and the off-shore islands more briefly under the heading OFF THE BEATEN TRACK. The areas where most of the tourist accommodation is situated are in the southeastern corner — Sanur, Nusa Dua and Kuta. The East, the area around Ubud, and the mountain locations are popular either for day trips or for excursions with one or two overnight stops. The same applies to the district we begin with, North Bali, nowadays somewhat neglected but once the gateway through which all visitors arrived on the island.

NORTH BALI

Northern Bali is in many ways distinct from the rest of the island. Whereas to the south the land falls away from the central mountains quite gently, creating the extensive fertile plains where most of the island's population lives, to the north the land drops more steeply to the coast, affording little easily cultivable ground. Temperatures, too, are slightly higher than in the south and the rainfall approximately half that of the southern plains.

Nevertheless, the very fact that the area is somewhat different is in itself an attraction. The abrupt descent of the land to the sea provides excellent views northward from temples perched on projecting spurs of land, the drier climate allows the cultivation of grapes, and the 7 km (4⅜ miles) beach-resort strip immediately west of Singaraja provides fine snorkeling and a peaceful ambiance that is very much to some people's taste.

Nowadays it is southern Bali that gets all the attention. With Denpasar as the island's administrative center, the airport at Tuban, and Kuta beach a mecca now that surfing has become the premier beach pleasure, the north hardly gets a look-in.

But it wasn't long ago that everything was based on Singaraja. When K'tut Tantri, the American expatriate who "went native," first established her glamorous and quickly famous international hotel at Kuta in the thirties, the site she chose was as far as it was possible to be from the center of operations of the colonial Dutch. Singaraja was their power-base and capital, largely because they had subdued northern Bali long before they extended their control to the south. International liners used the northern port (they now dock at Padang-

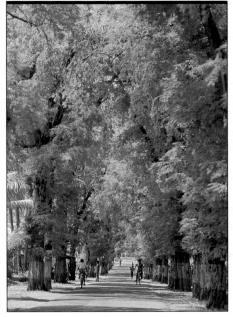

bai) and almost all foreign visitors arrived there.

Almost everyone nowadays arrives in north Bali by road from Denpasar via Bedugul. The 15-seater buses leave from the Ubung terminus. The fare Denpasar-Singaraja is Rp2,000, and the journey takes two hours. Travelers should not plan to leave Denpasar too late — buses are frequent up to 5 pm but you should check in advance at Ubung if you want to leave in the early evening. There are no buses during the night. Buses do not operate to set timeta-

North Bali is remote from the rest of the island — poorer, hotter and quieter. There are few tourists and all the accommodation is simple.

bles; they are privately operated and depart when they have recruited a full complement of passengers.

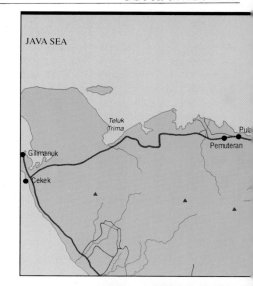

BALI'S OLD CAPITAL: SINGARAJA

Singaraja can seem an attractive enough place on a sunny morning, particularly from its upper streets commanding a view to the sea. But Bali is not a place that excels in its urban environments, and the truth is that there is very little to see in the town. The library, **Gedong Kirtya**, is said to contain a collection of Balinese manuscripts, sacred and other texts inscribed on palm leaves (*lontar*), but no one I know has ever found the place open. The **Tourist Information Bureau**, next door to the library on Jalan Veteran, seems a superfluous institution but is open most mornings.

Best is to see the town by night when the **Night Market** provides a dimly lit spectacle and adds a touch of glamor to a town that has little by day. When electricity is available, the market operates from 6 to 10 pm. On the frequent occasions when they have to make do with kerosene lamps things tend to end earlier. The many fruit sellers who set up at night along the main streets stay in business until midnight, however. One especially welcome feature of these stalls is the sale of apples, grown in the cooler mountain districts — to the embattled northerner suffering from a glut of tropical fruit, this is a blessing indeed. The market operates seven days a week, the two days of Nyepi (see THREE FESTIVALS, p.43) only excepted.

Virtually no foreign visitors actually stay in Singaraja as the attractive beach-side *losmen* and hotels of Lovina are only a 15-minute *bemo* ride away. Anyone intent on spending a night in the northern capital, however, might try the Duta Karya (☎ (0362) 21467; rates: moderate), three of whose 12 rooms have air-conditioning.

The celebrated Pura Beji at Sangsit: "sublime cosmic harmonies have become modulated into beautifully wrought shapes of pinkish-colored stone".

BLACK-SAND BEACHES: LOVINA

Lovina is the general term covering the black-sand beaches that extend from just before Anturan village, five minutes' drive west of Singaraja, to the far end of Kalibukbuk another couple of kilometers further down the road.

Ever since the development of Kuta, Sanur and Nusa Dua, Lovina has been a tranquil and almost forgotten retreat where you snorkeled by day and re-read a classic paperback by night. Today Lovina is expanding, but more slowly than the other tourist destinations on the island. It still retains a quiet, though no longer quite forgotten, air. In many ways it is reminiscent of what Sanur must have been like a couple of generations ago. Yet while many of the smaller homestays still have no phone, at the Singaraja end, new sparsely elegant establishments can·be found emerging incongruously from the rice paddies.

Despite these changes, the charm of Lovina for the moment still lies in its tranquility and its twin off-shore attractions, snorkeling along the reef, and the spectacle of dolphins at play just beyond it. Boatmen will be only too keen to take you out to experience either of these wonders.

Where to Stay

West to east, the **Parma Beach Homestay** (15 rooms; rates: inexpensive) is unassuming and serves large portions of homely food. The **Aditya** ((& fax 41059; 85 rooms; rates: moderate), by contrast, is a stylish establishment with a pool and a smart restaurant. A little further along, right on the beach, is one of the best and most popular places in Lovina, the **Nirwana** ((41288; 37 rooms; rates: inexpensive); goats chew the herbage and the wind rustles the palms. Meanwhile, those in search of something different might like the **Ayodya** (6 rooms; rates: inexpensive), a small colonial-style house with simple guest rooms in the garden.

Two of the better places at the Singaraja end are the **Banyualit Beach Inn** ((41889; fax 61563; 20 rooms, 6 with air-con; rates:

moderate) with its popular restaurant, and the recently upgraded **Baruna Beach Cottages** ((41252; fax 21108; 42 rooms; rates: moderate).

Characteristic of the newer hotels are the **Bali Lovina Beach Cottages** ((61478; fax 41385; 30 rooms; rates: moderate), the most expensive place in Lovina, the **Bali Taman Beach Hotel** ((41126; fax 41840; 18 rooms; rates: moderate) and the **Celuk Agung Beach Cottages** ((61379; 21 rooms; rates: moderate). Atmosphere at the last two is in rather short supply. A hotel larger than any currently in Lovina, the **Ganeca**, is due to open in the mid-1990's.

One of the bigger restaurants outside the hotels is the **Wina**, near the lane leading down to the Nirwana, while tasty food is also on offer at the small **Jasmine** restaurant opposite the Aditya. Lovina is even developing a nightlife — there is a nightclub of sorts, the **Malibu**, which serves food to the accompaniment of live music.

When contacting Lovina's hotels, note that the dialing code for North Bali is 0362.

SPRINGS AND TEMPLES

North Bali has several attractions besides those of the beach (which are limited, anyway, to the pleasures of snorkelling and underwater photography).

Fifty-six kilometers (35 miles) west from Singaraja on the coast road to Gilimanuk there is the **Pulaki Monkey Temple**. Sited on the road overlooking the sea, it is the home for hundreds of monkeys. Don't imagine, though, that you're doing them a favor when you buy them nuts from the ever-ready vendors — every local farm vehicle that passes empties out sackfuls of fruit oddments for them onto the road, an operation that makes the temple an inevitable slowing-down point for all traffic. It's in the nature of a religious offering, just as when *bemo* drivers pull up at shrines — no one is getting off, but the conductor (*kernet*) jumps down and places a tiny wicker tray of flowers and food there. The monkeys of Pulaki, sitting as often as not all over the road eating grapes and chunks of pineapple, are happy beings on the receiving end of the same pious devotion.

The Hot Springs at **Banjar**, 18 km (11¼ miles) west of Singaraja, is one of the nicest places in the north. Whereas before 1985 there were only muddy pools fed by water falling through bamboo pipes, now there is a modern complex worthy, albeit on a small scale, of Budapest or Baden-Baden. There are two tiled pools, one set above the other, into which a warm and slightly sulfurous stream of water gushes through magnificent dragon (*naga*) mouths.

even go by motorbike all the way from the main road.

A privately negotiated ride on the back of a bike is also the best way to get from the springs to the **Buddhist Temple**, Banjar's other attraction and something not to be missed. It's a walk through jungle of under a kilometer but it seems it's possible to lose your way; the motorbikes go by the road the long way round. (Rp500 for the one-way trip would be generous).

The temple is a beautiful mixture of Buddhist and Balinese Hindu elements.

There is a restaurant up above, and the whole ambiance, with its flowering shrubs and terraced garden overlooking the baths, is utterly delightful. It's rather like coming across the Emperor Nero's private retreat right in the middle of a tropical jungle.

To get there, ask the *bemo* driver for *air panas* at Banjar. You will be put down at a road junction where several horse-drawn traps (*dokar*) will be waiting to take you the 2 km (1¼ mile) drive up to the village (fare: Rp200). From there, a broad path leads off to the left, and 15 minutes' walk past rice paddies will bring you to the springs. It's impossible to get lost, but someone will take you on a motorbike if you ask (you will have to negotiate the fare). You can

Set on a steep hill overlooking the sea, it contains a lily pond, a yellow Buddha and numerous red-tiled roofs at different levels that make a most attractive combination. It's an easy walk back down to the coast road.

The falls at **Labuanhaji** are of less interest. A river forces its way through a cleft in the rocks and falls some 6 m (19½ ft) into a murky pool. There is another fall and pool above, accessible by a slippery path.

Whereas it's certain that after heavy rain these waterfalls would be more impressive, nevertheless, given their modest

Black sand, fishing nets, the shore serving as a major footpath — the lonely coast of North Bali.

scale and the lack of any facilities (in contrast to Banjar), they are barely worth the 1½ km (⅞ mile) trudge from the road. If you do go, boys will press their services on you as "guides," in effect showing you where to turn off the lane and take the short brick path beside the paddy.

UNHEARD MELODIES

Eight kilometers (5 miles) east of Singaraja is the celebrated **Pura Beji** at **Sangsit**. It is one of the most elaborately carved temples in all Bali, so much so that carved wings stand right out, all but free from the mother stone.

In the clammy silence, the smiling faces of the men and gods gaze out in voluptuous ease, caught forever in a moment of serene resignation. The peace and infinite generosity of Balinese Hinduism is wonderfully expressed here in this gorgeous place. "Heard melodies are sweet," wrote the English poet Keats, "but those unheard are sweeter." Here at Pura Beji the most sublime cosmic harmonies have become modulated into beautifully wrought shapes of pinkish-colored stone.

The temple is not difficult to find. A small sign points the way downhill off Sangsit's main street, but anyone will show you the way — it's the only place in this little agricultural market any visitor ever goes to.

GONGS

Sawan, another 9 km (5⅝ miles) east, is a most attractive village. It's known as the place where gongs for *gamelan* orchestras are fired — just say "gong" and any child will lead you up a lane and through a barn door, and there they will be, a couple of men and a woman hammering, polishing and working bellows for the fire.

But the real charm lies in just wandering through this very restful place, taking lunch at a street-side *warung*, and watching the easy, tranquil village life go by. Sawan is reached by *bemo* from the main road between Sangsit and Kubutambahan, passing the village of **Jagaraga** on the way up (fare: Rp300).

The temple at Kubutambahan is at the junction of the road from Kintamani and the coast road. Most visitors give the place only a couple of minutes — time enough to photograph the carving of a man on a flowery bicycle: the guardian will show you where it is once you have signed the visitors' book and paid your donation.

YEH SANIH

At Yeh Sanih, another 6 km (3¾ miles) east, freshwater springs have been diverted to create bathing pools between the road and the sea. There's an accompanying restaurant and accommodation, **Bungalow Puri Sanih** (rates: inexpensive). Frogs croak, mosquitoes bite, and boys flop into the cool water.

The coast, as elsewhere in north Bali, has a rather bleak appearance. The bungalow rooms are satisfactory, and there's a small temple up a short path on the other side of the road. You might be lucky when you visit it to hear a strange and beautiful

OPPOSITE and ABOVE: The Buddhist temple at Banjar. Buddhist elements coexist with the dominant Hinduism without abrasion — there are, for example, Buddhist *pedanda* (high priests) as well as Hindu ones.

whistling and tinkling in the air — a few members of a local bird orchestra out for a quick run-through of a small part of their repertoire.

VILLAGE WITH A VIEW

Sembiran is a large village 3 km (1⅞ miles) up from the road. The road is good, but transport is by motorbike — a group of them wait at the junction for prospective customers (Rp500 should be considered a maximum fare).

The village itself is rather neglected though it was clearly once important. Visitors are few, and children run away startled as you approach. What is very fine about Sembiran, though, is the temple perched on the hillside 1 km (⅝ mile) before you get to the village proper. Your transport will wait for you while you take a couple of pictures, but don't linger too long as other fares are waiting and he will not be slow to urge you on. Best, perhaps, is to walk back down from the village (the temple will be on your left) and inspect it at your leisure.

Characteristically of north Bali, the site commands an excellent view out over the sea, though technically, like all Balinese temples, it is oriented upwards to the mountains. Trimly kept, the place has an almost Greek atmosphere, and its gray stone and green grass give it a simplicity which is classical.

SANUR

A DISCREET CAMPARI

Sanur is altogether a very comfortable place —not cheap, but long-established, leafy and reassuring. The beach may not be up to Kuta's but then no beach in Bali is. You are in Indonesia, just about, when you are in Sanur, whereas in Nusa Dua further south, despite all their attempts to prove the contrary, you could be on the moon.

All the hotels, except the Bali Beach Hotel and the Bali Hyatt, are of the bungalow type and are often set in shady tropical gardens, most of them fronting onto the beach, which is generally quite safe. Snorkeling is available off a sheltered reef that stretches out from the yellow sands and colorful fishing boats. There are fine views east with the mountains of central Bali rising grandly across the bay.

All the tourist facilities available in such profusion in Kuta are here too, but presented in a more genteel, affluent way. Sanur is a lush garden where visitors lie on beach beds under palm trees sipping their Camparis or flop splendidly into a pool. (Hotels without pools can't really compete in Sanur.) Leather traveling bags replace canvas ones. It's as discreet, worldly and wise as Kuta is fresh, brash and innocent. You pay your money — rather more than in Kuta, but less than in Nusa Dua — and you take your choice.

WHERE TO STAY

Almost all the more exclusive hotels in Sanur are right on the beach. Starting from the north and working south, you'll come across **Alit's Beach Bungalows** (℡ 8567 and 8560; 98 rooms; rates: average and above). The hotel is situated where the continuation of the road from Denpasar arrives at the sea. Just carry straight on after the traffic lights, leaving the grand entrance to the grounds of the Bali Beach Hotel on your right. All rooms have air-con and hot running water and there is a swimming pool.

The **Bali Beach Hotel** (℄ 88511; fax 87917; 605 rooms; rates: expensive) probably has every facility anyone is likely to require. It's the only hotel outside Nusa Dua built upwards rather than in the more usual bungalow/garden style, but it also has its low-rise wing and cottages. You approach the hotel down a long drive with a nine-hole golf-course on the right, where

figures in white tropical suits swing their clubs with Balinese caddies in attendance. A gamelan orchestra celebrates your arrival for lunch, and many of the airlines are in the process of establishing offices in the hotel to facilitate your smooth departure.

The **Segara Village Hotel** (℄ 88407; fax 87242; 150 rooms; rates: expensive) with two-story cottages in garden surroundings, is quiet and relaxing, and fronts onto the beach. It has special programs and facilities for children.

In Sanur, eyes of tourist and local alike are turned seaward.

A slightly less expensive hotel, still on the sea front, is the **Natour Sindhu Beach Hotel** (℄ 88351; fax 89268; 59 rooms; rates: average and above).

Continuing south, the **Hotel Tandjung Sari** (℄ 88441; fax 87930; 30 rooms; rates: expensive) is the preferred hideaway for celebrities and jet-setters in Sanur. For many it is the place to stay in Bali. Meanwhile the **Santrian Beach Cottages** (℄ 88009; fax 87101;134 rooms; rates: average and above) offer the usual one-and two-story bungalows in the usual verdant tropical gardens.

The **Bali Hyatt** (℄ 88361; fax 87693; 387 rooms; rates: expensive), set in an astonishing 15 hectares (36 acres) of land, combines very Balinese public areas with four-story accommodation. High thatched roofs rise over restaurants serving food from Indonesia and Italy, and sauna and disco complete the international-yet-in-Bali ambiance.

Lastly, at the far end of the beach the **Sanur Beach Hotel** (℄ 88011; fax 87566; 425 rooms; rates: expensive) claims to be the friendliest of the big Sanur hotels. It's recently been renovated and is usually booked solid by tour groups.

As you might except, the cheaper accommodation tends to be back from the beach, but it's never very far. Sanur does not specialize in facilities for budget travelers, but the **Taman Agung Inn** (℄ 88549; 13 rooms; rates: moderate) is one of a handful of places in this category.

WHERE TO EAT

Sanur looks as if it teems with restaurants. This is because, like the hotels, they all crowd together along the one road running just inland from the beach, Jalan Tanjung Sari. An exception is the new and very fashionable **Cafe Batu Jimbar** (℄ 84374) on Jalan Danau Tamblingan. Other popular places include the **Italian Terrazzo Martini** (℄ 88371), the **Legong Restaurant** (℄ 88066; fax 33386) with European, Chinese and Indonesial food, and Balinese dancers performing at dinner time, the amiable and cosy **Mandelo's** (℄ 88773), and **Ronnie's Pub and Restaurant** (℄ 88370) with live music several nights a week.

The **Karya Bar and Restaurant** ((88376) is another of Sanur's many stylish restaurants. There's a wide choice of cuisines, with live music or dance most nights. Transport is provided from local hotels — just give them a ring. There's a Japanese restaurant, too, the **Kita** ((88158), serving, among other dishes, *sukiyaki, tempura and yakitori*. Note that it closes at 10 pm.

The further south you go in Sanur, once you're past the Hyatt, the cheaper it gets. After the road becomes a dirt track there are a number of very reasonable warung, bars and small restaurants to be found.

NIGHTLIFE

Nightlife is not a prominent feature of Sanur as most people make for the charismatic venues at Kuta, only a fifteen minute drive away. There is **Number One**, however, at Batu Jimbar, the name for the southern end of Sanur. Telephone them on 88097 and they'll send a car for you. It's a smart place: no shorts, thongs (flip-flops) or singlets. Considering this is precisely the attire most holiday-makers in Bali wear all the time, this constitutes some requirement. There's also **Subec** on Jalan Tanjung Sari, and the **Matahari** in the Bali Hyatt.

SHOPPING

Souvenir and art shops of the classier kind are a feature of Sanur, and **Keramik Jenggala** at Batu Jimbar is an excellent place for pottery.

In addition, there are shopping arcades at the bigger Sanur hotels such as the Bali Hyatt and the Hotel Bali Beach. Prices here, however, are above those in many of the small shops elsewhere on the island.

AN EXPLOSION OF PAINT

One of the few historical sites in Sanur is the house, now known as the **Museum Le Mayeur**, where the Belgian painter Le Mayeur lived from 1932 to 1958. The place has been left more or less as it was, with his books still on his desk and so on. What is so striking about the house is that his

painting explodes from the framed pictures onto the walls and eventually all over the window frames. Fantastic scenes from the *Ramayana* epic in augmented Balinese style feature prominently. There are several rooms, and plans are afoot to restore the building before the effects of the tropical climate cause it to deteriorate still further.

It's the daughter of Le Mayeur's Balinese wife who shows you round, and she also runs the small establishment adjacent to the house called the **Pollok Art Shop**. This stocks a well-chosen mixture of items: silver jewelry, wood-carvings, batik, some paintings, T-shirts — a range that makes it possible to shop for souvenirs and presents all in one place and avoid the need to tramp at length in the heat to different shops round the district.

BALI'S CAPITAL: DENPASAR

Denpasar is emphatically not an attractive place. It is Bali's capital, but few tourists have any need to go there, and there are few good reports of it from people who have been and escaped back to Kuta or Sanur to tell the tale. There are, for instance, numerous small hotels and losmen there, but it's rare that anyone other than Indonesians from outside Bali on business in Denpasar stays in them.

It's a crowded, noisy, polluted town, the very antithesis of everything people come to Bali to find. Like many another Asian city, it's caught between two moments in history; it was built for an age of horse-drawn or pedestrian traffic and now endures the full force of modern mechanized transport.

So great is the tourist concentration in Kuta and Sanur that even shopping and such services as banks, telex offices and travel agents are as good there as in Denpasar, or better. A visit to the Immigration Office, or the Denpasar Police Office to get a license to drive a motorbike on Bali if you don't have an international driver's license, is the most likely reason for paying a visit to the town.

Nevertheless, Denpasar does have one or two places of interest and these will be dealt with briefly here.

HEROIC LAST STAND

The center of Denpasar can be said to be a large grassy square known as the **Tanah Lapang Puputan Badung**. Its notable feature is a heroic, three-figure statue standing in pools amid fountains, a memorial to the four thousand Balinese who died defending the city against the Dutch on September 20, 1906.

Standing facing the monument from the center of the square, the building on your right is the **Museum Bali**, with the Pura Jagatnatha next to it on the left. Over on the opposite side of the square is the military headquarters for the island.

Frankly, for a place with the cultural significance of Bali, the museum is a bit of a joke. The basic concept, that its very buildings should in themselves be exhibits of Balinese temple and palace architectural styles, is attractive. But unfortunately the contents have neither the range, nor are they labeled clearly and in sufficient languages, to make them the major resource such an institution really ought to house.

Exhibits include a model of a tooth-filing ceremony, some interesting masks, some paintings and wood-carvings and a display of agricultural tools and implements. There is no catalog available in English.

The museum is open from 8am to 5pm daily, except on Fridays when it closes at 3:30pm, and Mondays when it is closed all day.

The **Pura Jagatnatha** is a modern temple dedicated to the whole of Bali. Unlike most Balinese temples, it is closed to the public except at festival times.

ART AND INFORMATION

Two art centers provide useful indications of what riches the island has in store. The **National Art Center**, between Jalan Abiankapas and Jalan Palawa Pagan in the east of the town, contains exhibits of shadow puppets and the giant *barong landong* puppets, silverware, carvings, basketry, paintings and weaving. Further east — you'll need to take a taxi — is the government-run, fixed-price art shop; ask the driver for **Sanggraha Kriya Asta**. It not only has a wide range of items but it also provides a convenient indication of the kind of prices to be paid for similar objects elsewhere when you will be expected to bargain for them.

You can attend lessons in Balinese dance at two places in Denpasar. One is the **Academy of Dance, Indonesia** (otherwise known as ASTI) on Jalan Nusa Indah. The other is the **Conservatory of Performing Arts** (otherwise known as KOKAR) — check with the Badung Tourist Office for the location of this one as they were about to move at the time of writing. Lessons at each institution take place in the mornings.

There is a six-week long annual **Bali Arts Festival** between mid-June and the end of July at the Werdi Budaya Arts Center, Jalan Nusa Indah.

The **Badung Government Tourist Office** at Merdeka Building, 7 Jalan Surapati (℄ 23399 and 23602), provides maps, lists of festivals (valuable as these go by the Balinese calendar and so vary from year to year) and details of dance and other performances. It's not the full service provided by some countries but the attendants are helpful and do respond to personal inquiries. The office is open from 7 am to 2 pm daily, except on Friday it closes at 11 am and Monday it is shut all day.

The **Bali Government Tourist Office**, by contrast, is difficult to find, being located in a complex of government buildings, and not really oriented to the needs of the individual inquirer. If, however, you think you need them, they're at Jalan S. Parman, Niti Mandala Renon (℄ 22387 and 26313).

Should you happen to hold a visa of the kind that can be renewed (see TRAVELERS' TIPS for information on visas), then you may need to go to the **Immigration Office** (Kantor Imigrasi). It's in the Renon Complex, Niti Mandala. It's open from 7 am to 1 pm, except on Friday when it closes at 11 am, Saturday when it closes at 12 noon, and Sunday when it's shut.

WHERE TO STAY

If you need for any reason to stay in Denpasar, one of the following should suit your needs. The best hotel in town is the **Natour Bali** (℄ 5681-3; fax 35347; 75 rooms; rates: average and above). It's the old Dutch colonial hotel (Charlie Chaplin and Noel Coward among many other celebrities stayed there), and though now over fifty years old it has been tastefully modernized, and has a swimming pool and an ambiance that manages to be both efficient and relaxed. It's located at Jalan Veteran 3.

The **Pamecutan Palace**, (℄ 23491, 44 rooms, rates: average and above) at Jalan Thamrin 2 is also reasonable.

A smaller, homely place is the **Wismasari Inn** (℄ 22437; 14 rooms; rates: moderate) at Jalan Majen Sutoyo 1. Rooms are very clean and reasonably comfortable.

WHERE TO EAT

Food in Denpasar tends to be Indonesian as foreign tourists are not that common.

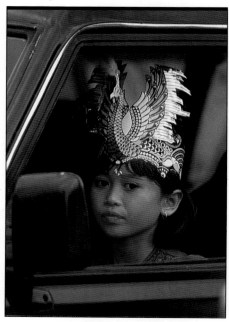

The Natour Bali, however, provides a varied cuisine.

SHOPPING

Most of Denpasar's major shops are situated on Jalan Gajah Mada, but if you're using public transport you'll have to walk there as *bemos* are not allowed to drive along it. A selection of books on Bali in English can be seen at the **Corsica Bookshop** on Jalan Sumatra.

TRANSPORT

There are three main *bemo* stations in Denpasar, **Tegal**, **Ubung** and **Batubulan**. Each

OPPOSITE: The Nusa Dua Hotel, one of the handful of five-star hostelries in this ultra-exclusive enclave; all have international-standard facilities as well as sharing some sporting amenities. ABOVE: A young celebrant heads home after a festival; Mas.

serves a different area of the island, and little three-wheel *bemo*s shuttle back and forth between them for a few hundred rupiah a ride. They also run to **Kereneng**, the home station for *bemo*s plying routes within Denpasar.

Tegal serves Kuta, the airport, Ulu Watu and Nusa Dua (should anyone staying at Nusa Dua ever want to use a *bemo*). Ubung serves the west and north; mini-buses leave from here to Gilimanuk and Singaraja/Lovina. Batubulan is the station for services to Ubud, Kintamani

NUSA DUA AND THE BUKIT

IN PRAISE OF LIMESTONE

The region south of the airport is generally referred to as the Bukit. It is the Balinese word for hill and strictly refers only to the high ground southwest of Nusa Dua. Nevertheless, the whole peninsula is of a piece, and the reason is that whereas the rest of mainland Bali is made up of volcanic rock and soils, the Bukit, like the nearby offshore

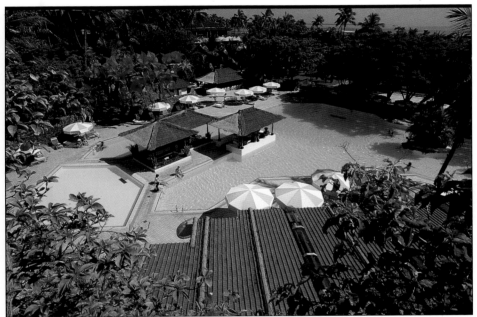

and East Bali. For a *bemo* to Sanur, go to Kereneng.

A further small station, **Sanglah**, serves Benoa Harbor.

One final point — all over Bali you will hear *bemo* drivers touting for passengers calling out "*Badung!*" In fact, "*Badung, Badung!*" rings through the dusty evening air from Klungkung to Kuta, from Ubud to Tabanan. You won't find it on any map, but just as Karangasem is the old Balinese name for Amlapura, and Buleleng for Singaraja, Badung is the name by which all Balinese know the Denpasar area, and these tired and hungry drivers are looking for their last fares of the day before finally heading home.

island of Nusa Penida, is entirely limestone. Indeed, it is probable that at one time the Bukit was once an island too: even today it is only connected to Bali proper by a low-lying and rather narrow isthmus.

Rainwater runs straight into the ground in limestone country, and the consequent lack of surface streams means there is no water available for irrigation during the dry season. As a result, in the Bukit life has traditionally been hard. The selection of Nusa Dua (literally Two Islands) for development as a major tourist complex has done little to alter the traditional life of the region.

The area includes the five-star complex of Nusa Dua itself, the fishing village of

Tanjung Benoa sited at the end of a five kilometer sand strip directly to the north of Nusa Dua, the village and bay of Jimbaran (located on the neck of the isthmus immediately south of the airport) and the upland area itself that culminates in the magnificently sited temple and surfing venues of Ulu Watu.

FIVE-STAR LUXURY

The development of Nusa Dua only really got under way in the early eighties. Prior to that, the area was an infertile coastal patch featuring the two small "islands," connected to the mainland by sandy strips, which give the place its name.

Nusa Dua's hotels are all five-star and each in its own style is the last word in luxury. All come up to the highest international standards and stand in their own ample grounds complete with several restaurants, swimming pools, etc. Indeed, each of them is a self-sufficient holiday environment, and anything that might be thought to be missing — Balinese local culture, for instance — is brought in and presented for the hotel guests' exclusive delectation.

Nusa Dua's beaches may not be the finest on the island but they are safe and adequate to many people's needs. They are sheltered behind reefs, so are shallow and placid, and they have white sand. Rocks and seaweed become more common as you move south, so that Club Med enjoys the best beach and the Grand Hyatt the least good. On none of them are you likely to meet people other than fellow guests at the Nusa Dua hotels. To some people, however, this is a positive advantage, and certainly anyone concerned about security can be confident that here they are staying in a place specially designed with their safety in mind. Along the long avenues of palms that link the access roads to the hotels, security men are stationed on their motorbikes, lolling in boredom across the handlebars of their machines. Their main function in normal times seems to be to keep hawkers away from these wide acres in which are concentrated many of the richest people staying on Bali at any one moment.

The atmosphere created by well-trimmed verges and impeccable tarred driveways is more that of a presidential golf-course than somewhere given over to free-and-easy relaxation. And indeed the **Nusa Dua Beach Hotel** (℡ 71210; fax 71229; 450 rooms; rates: expensive) is where heads of state stay when they visit Indonesia, government officials flying down from Jakarta to meet them here rather than having to face the security nightmare presented by the nation's capital. The Reagans stayed there, in a presidential suite "with special security features," in 1986, and in many ways the whole district, with access confined to a narrow bottleneck close to the airport, is ideal for such uses. Nusa Dua as a whole was conceived as an environment in which world statesmen could meet, and tourists subsequently pay for the honor of breathing the air of the same prestigious environment. The architectural style of the Nusa Dua Beach Hotel is solidly generous, while its rooms are in four-story blocks.

The **Melia Bali Sol** (℡ 71510; fax 71360; 500 rooms; rate: expensive), by contrast, mixes tropical and Spanish styles in its conception; it too has rooms in four-story blocks.

The **Putri Bali** (℡ 71020 and 71420; fax 71139; 425 rooms; rates: expensive) is the other big, traditional hotel at Nusa Dua. The name means "Balinese Princess."

The **Bali Club Med** (℡ 71520; fax 71831; 350 rooms; rates: expensive) offers a very different kind of vacation. Three extensive buffet meals a day, all sports equipment and instruction, and supervised activities for children, plus a cabaret show every night, are provided for the inclusive price. Yet you can ignore it all if you like and simply use the place like any other luxury hotel — and this is the most luxurious of Club Med's Asian properties.

The forecourt of the **Bali Hilton International** (℡ 71102; fax 71199; 540 rooms; rates: expensive) resembles a grandiose pleasure palace Ghenghis Khan never had time to build. Statues gesture gesture extravagantly across multi-level waterfalls in a determined attempt to out-do even Nusa Dua's general exclusivity.

The **Grand Hyatt Bali** (℃ 71188; fax 71084; 750 rooms; rates: expensive) similarly opts for the Grand Hotel style, though on a slightly more human scale. A swimming maze, including slides and shutes, makes up for the less than ideal beach.

The **Nusa Indah** (℃ 71906; fax 71908; 400 rooms; rates: expensive) doubles as Indonesia's most up-to-date convention center, while the smaller **Sheraton Lagoon** (℃ 71327; fax 71326; 275 rooms; rates: expensive) offers an intimacy that tends to be missed elsewhere.

The smallest of Nusa Dua's hotels is the **Hotel Bualu** (℃ 71310; fax 71313; 50 rooms; rates: expensive). It is well-suited to children, has a PADI diving instructor and free sporting facilities.

Finally, overlooking Nusa Dua is the ultra-luxurious and exclusive **Amanusa** (℃ 72332; fax 72335; 35 suites; rates: from US$270), the sister of the Amandari at Ubud and the Amankila near Candi Dasa. It is classically beautiful and commands stunning views.

Also at Nusa Dua is the **Bali Golf and Country Club** (℃ 71791; fax 71797), with an

18-hole golf course of championship standard. Green fees are currently US$77, but some hotels include use of its facilities as part of a package.

UNEXPECTED BENOA

Benoa is actually the name for the port of Denpasar; the fishing village that faces it from the other side of the bay is Tanjung Benoa. It's a longish way round from one to the other by road, but a short trip by boat. Between the two, sheltering the en-

trance to the bay, lies Pulau Serangan, commonly known to tour operators as Turtle Island.

It is the fishing village that's most likely to interest visitors. It's an unexpected place, slightly down-market with a raffish, freewheeling air, like somewhere long forgotten but determined to stand up for itself. But the development of nearby Nusa Dua has seen a string of new hotels along the road joining the two places, and Benoa is now an important center for diving, parasailing and wind-surfing.

Sea, Sun and Food

Equipment and boats are available from **Beluga** (℡ 71767; fax 71146), while the **Rai Seafood Restaurant** (℡ 72012) is the best place to eat, an attractive establishment that fetches you free of charge from any Nusa Dua

ABOVE: Tourists enjoying a ride on a *prahu* off Sanur. OPPOSITE: These enthusiasts are on their way across the shallow strait to the temple on Pulau Serangan on the occasion of its anniversary celebration (*odalan*), held every 210 days.

hotel, rents out equipment and arranges tours by sea. There is a wonderful view in the late afternoon across the strait to the sun-etched cliffs of Nusa Penida.

Transport can be arranged from Benoa's harbor over to Turtle Island. In addition, the village has an important and recently renovated Chinese temple.

TURTLE ISLAND

Pulau Serangan (Turtle Island) is a low, sandy spit only cut off from the mainland to the north at high tide. Variations in tidal levels, however, make it inadvisable to cross other than by boat. The island is covered by palm trees and at its one village turtles are kept in pens being fattened up for sale on the "mainland." You can charter a small boat to take you across from either the northern or southern side — from the southern, Nusa Dua side, the cost is likely to be around Rp7,000 there and back per boatload, with room for several people. The island is a popular destination for half-day tours from Kuta and you'll probably have a nicer time if you plan your trip early in the morning or at the end of the afternoon to avoid coinciding with one of these.

A FISHING BEACH

The village of **Jimbaran**, which straddles the road running south from close by the airport to Ulu Watu, is currently poised to be destroyed by the tourist industry.

Coming from Kuta, after passing the stalls of the village market, a road leaves off to the right where tall *kepuh* trees mark the site of a cemetery where bodies awaiting cremation are buried. This leads to the beach and the friendly yet modern **Hotel Puri Bali** (℡ 52605; fax 52220; 41 rooms; rates: expensive), until recently the only hotel in this area.

Now, however, there is also the **Keraton Bali Cottages** (℡ 53991; fax 53881; 99 rooms; rates: expensive), a luxurious establishment fronting onto the road and backing onto the beach, and in addition a Regent and a gigantic Intercontinental are under construction at the south end of the bay, the

latter all set to dominate the shapely peninsula. How much more of this kind of thing Bali can take without being fundamentally changed for the worse is a question that the spectacle of Jimbaran inevitably poses.

Jimbaran Bay itself is sandy, with fishing boats pulled up on the beach, and the airport runway visible at the northern end, the waiting planes silhouetted against the sky.

From Jimbaran, the road, after crossing level country, begins to climb up onto the

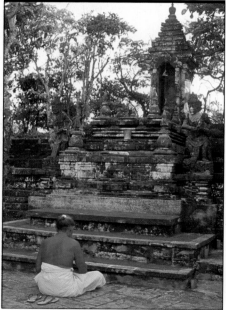

limestone plateau itself, and before long there is a fine view backwards over the airport and southern Bali. Immediately piles of white stone, destined for the most part for roadworks, can be seen at the side of the road. With its dry stone walls and scanty vegetation, the landscape looks like what geographers refer to as karst scenery anywhere in the world. Underground there may be secret rivers and caverns measureless to man, but on the surface the soft dry contours present a terser, tighter-lipped picture. In place of lush rice terraces and coconut palms is a waterless landscape more reminiscent, with its chirping crickets and scent of herbs, of the south of France than the tropics.

The red-tiled buildings you pass on the left are the premises of Denpasar's **Universitas Udayana**. Two kilometers (1¼ miles) further on, ignore a left turn at a small junction with a statue if your destination is Ulu Watu, the road to which offers beautiful glimpses of the sea ahead, until finally it arrives, 21 km (14 miles) from Kuta, at its destination.

TEMPLE ABOVE THE STONE

After passing a *warung* on the right, the road swings sharply to the left and terminates in a car park where food and drink is also available. This car park serves **Pura Luhur Ulu Watu**, one of Bali's six Temples of the World and one of the finest places on the whole island.

A wide path takes you down an incline, and then the long flight of steps of the temple itself is ahead of you. The silence, the dry, scented air and the proximity of the sea fill you with an almost unbearable expectation.

Luhur Ulu Watu probably means Above the Stone, and this is just what it is. The temple is built on a high ledge of rock extending out over the sea 76 m (250 ft) below. Nothing could be more dramatic, or more beautiful. On three sides the Indian Ocean rolls in with some of the biggest waves in Asia. Java is just visible straight ahead. The gods stare out in their usual sublime comprehension, but here, with all the power of nature at their feet, their serenity is doubly authentic. The white of the limestone they're carved in and the blue of the sea combine unforgettably in this pure and special place.

The temple goes back at least a thousand years and probably more. The sixteenth-century Buddhist sage Wawu Rauh is said to have achieved *moksa* (or attained Nirvana) here. Nothing could be less surprising.

Beware of Monkeys

There is only one small practical note that needs to be sounded in the general air of

ABOVE and OPPOSITE: Pura Luhur, Ulu Watu and its somewhat sacred monkeys.

ecstasy and sublime transcendance. The temple is inhabited by a small band of very mischievous monkeys. They will not pause for a moment's thought before jumping down and seizing any item you leave unguarded, knowing that you will try to trick them into letting you get it back with offers of food. In the process your camera or wallet could very well be dropped from one of the trees, where the monkeys usually retire, into the sea. The temple attendants say that this is a common occurrence. So be warned — but don't allow an excessive concern for your possessions to distract you from the full wonder of being where you are.

SURFING MECCA

The **Ulu Watu** that is such a special place for Bali's surfers is hardly less impressive. To get there, take the road from the car park as if you're heading to Kuta, but stop at the *warung* a couple of hundred meters down on your left. Leave any four-wheeled vehicle you may have with you in the car park — the only way down the 2 km (1¼miles) to the coast is by motorbike or on foot. The path leaves the road just by the warung, and there are always boys there with motorbikes waiting to take you.

The way descends slowly between prickly pear cactus hedges. Shortly after the place where the bikes wait to bring people back, you go down some concrete steps into a dry valley. From here you can climb down a short bamboo ladder into the so-called cave (actually its roof has collapsed) that leads to the cove, or follow the path up to the line of *warung* and souvenir stalls that the enterprising Balinese have established on the steep sides of the slope overlooking the ocean.

There's not much to be seen from the little cove itself, just to the left of where the cave meets the sea. The sand is gritty and the sea bed rocky, but at least it's a place to get wet and cool off, and someone will even try to sell you a silver amulet. The really wonderful place is the highest of the *warung*.

This is perched on the edge of a ridge running up the cliff and commands a stupendous view out over the incoming surf. The spectacle is quite extraordinary. The sea is spread out before you in all its majestic fury away to the right Agung is outlined — on a good day — against the blue. You can sit there under the *warung*'s thatched roof and sip your iced fruit juice and watch the figures far below skimming along the great glassy slopes as if they were on skis, playing with the ocean like children in the vast lap of the gods. And as the sun goes down, straight ahead of you, it shines through the waves like light coming through the green stained-glass windows of a cathedral.

Together, the temple and this surfing location make Ulu Watu among the very finest places in all Bali.

KUTA

YELLOW SANDS AND TECHNICOLOR SUNSETS

Kuta Beach extends in a long and gentle curve from just north of the airport through Kuta proper, then Legian, to the Bali Oberoi Hotel at Seminyak and beyond. The sand is fine, hard-packed and yellow, and the surf that breaks along the length of the beach originates somewhere near the Antarctic and is famous worldwide. So too are Kuta's sunsets. It is far and away Bali's finest beach.

AN EXOTIC FAIRGROUND

Kuta is in every possible way the diametric opposite to, for instance, Nusa Dua. Its development was unplanned. It is in many places ramshackle. Very cheap food and accommodation are available everywhere. There are touts on every hand, and at the south end of the beach barely five minutes pass without someone approaching you to sell you a T-shirt or give you a massage. To some people this is an intolerable intrusion, even though you do not have to walk very far in the direction of Legian to avoid most or all of this attention.

But the fact remains that, in addition to its supremely magnificent beach, Kuta teems with irrepressible life. The beach scene at the southern airport end resembles nothing so much as a circus, but it's the circus of democratic life in the late twentieth century and is, in many ways, something not to be missed. It's doubtful if there's anywhere else in the world quite like it.

Australian grannies, who no doubt live very modestly back home in Adelaide, can be seen surrounded by a veritable court of hair braiders, hair beaders, massage artists, runners bearing iced beer from the

leled magnet to Balinese for whom tourism represents an opportunity to make profits unheard of in other departments of the island's life. Everyone thinks he has a bargain at Kuta, and the result is a fairground of happy buying and enthusiastic selling, all under the glorious sun on one of Asia's most fabulous beaches.

The essential difference between Kuta and the more exclusive resorts to the east is that at Kuta the tourists and the local population interact by and large as individuals. This is not to say that the one

beach restaurants, sellers of Dyak elixirs fresh from the jungles of Borneo — add an Italian tenor and it would be the levee scene from the opera *Der Rozenkavalier.*

Yet a few hundred meters away a hundred or more Balinese may be performing a post-cremation ceremony involving a procession in full traditional dress and the scattering of ashes on the waves accompanied by the release onto the waters of ducks, chickens and doves.

The key to it all is that while Kuta remains an extraordinarily cheap and "exotic" holiday destination for the huge numbers of Australians, Japanese, Germans, French, British and many others who flock there, this same conglomeration is an unparal-

group is not very much more advantaged than the other. But whereas elsewhere most of the Balinese you will encounter will be employees of hotel syndicates, and acting out essentially the roles of servants, in Kuta the majority will be in one way or another in business on their own behalf.

This applies too, and indeed particularly, to the accommodation scene. Because Kuta grew without official planning, many of the businesses in the area remain in local hands. Thus the profusion of small, budget-price *losmen* is no coincidence: they exist because Kuta grew from

An international crowd waits for the sunset on Kuta beach, December. Sometimes the great event refuses to happen on cue, but sometimes ...

travelers in the sixties arriving at what was then only a medium-sized village and asking to be provided with food and a place to stay. First-class hotels have, of course, moved in since that time, and it would be a great mistake to think that Kuta only offers budget facilities. But this makes Kuta even more of a democratic phenomenon than it would otherwise have been. All tastes and all bank balances are catered for. All the world comes to Kuta Beach, and almost all Bali, it sometimes seems, is waiting there to greet them.

constantly being polished, children offering to bring you ice-cold drinks for Rp200 commission, one elderly lady bearing ancient *lontar* (strips of palm leaf inscribed with sacred texts), and the inevitable and welcome sellers of hats and beach mats.

Midday sees a dramatic diminution, most of the Balinese retreating from the sun's ferocious glare and only clutches of sun-drunk northerners remaining to play frisbee relentlessly before collapsing in one of the beach bars for protracted lunches of seafood, beer and grainy Indonesian coffee

A DAY IN THE SUN

The day on the beach follows a regular cycle. The Surf Rescue take up their positions at 6 am and even then there are the early morning joggers and before-breakfast swimmers. By nine the beach is filling up and many of the suntan zealots are already in place. Soon the colorful scene is at the first of its two daily heights; the beach traders are all at work: boys with a single wood-carving wrapped in its cloth and

to the sound of some of the older Australian and American pop hits.

If often the afternoon seems slow to take off, it's no doubt because the morning went on so long, and sunset here in the tropics is anyway very early. This, you quickly realize, is why the Indonesians get up at 4 am — in this land of eternal summer, light is gone by 5.45 in the afternoon.

THE SUNSET EVENT

Kuta's sunsets were renowned even in K'tut Tantri's day (see BIBLIOGRAPHY), and nowadays, as the coaches pull up from Nusa Dua's five-star hotels, all of Kuta, from its tattooed Japanese surfers to its

Kuta's sunset — "the great Indian Ocean surf laps as if entranced" — and some people are reluctant to call it a day.

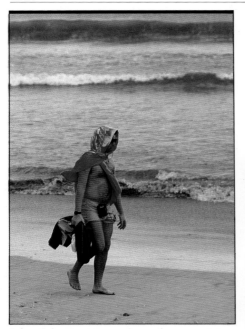

Jakarta businessmen down for a week by the sea, set up their cameras where they will best catch the reflection on the wet sand, and wait.

The event itself is very like a prima-donna's performance in opera — maybe the miracle will happen, maybe it won't. Sometimes Great Nature has a cough and, despite cloudless skies, the sun sinks with no more attendant glory than a fifty-cent piece dropped into a puddle. But some-times, ah, sometimes... then the beams shoot up like chiseled shafts, the colors deepen through apricot to salmon to a final consummating crimson, the great Indian Ocean surf laps as if entranced, and the planes drift in to land stage-right like windblown stars. And all at once it's night. The moon has established her quiet sover-eignty above the palms, the motorbikes — mere spots of light — putter across the sand, plying their night trade, and the audience disperses to supper, and other pleasures and diversions.

Kuta — "the circus of democratic life in the late twentieth century". ABOVE LEFT: Heard melodies. ABOVE RIGHT: Hair beaders at work. OPPOSITE LEFT: The clothes market on Jalan Bakungsari. OPPOSITE RIGHT: Hats and mats for sale.

A MEETING OF CULTURES

And on Sundays the Balinese themselves come down to savor some of the relaxing activities being enjoyed by the foreigners, those lords from other lands who are able to have what they will probably never know, holidays lasting seven days in a week. They set up goal posts on the sands

or wade tentatively into the ocean still, in many cases, wearing knee-length dresses. Or else they simply gaze from above the high-water mark, in their polished Sunday shoes, at the splendor and luxury before them.

Inland, Kuta resembles a Hollywood set for a cut-price Western. A couple of paces behind the single-story facade of boutiques and restaurants is another world, one of pastoral *losmen*, coconut groves, tethered cattle and free-ranging poultry. Take your choice which is stranger — the magical world of the immemorial pastoral round or the tacked-together world of Kuta's main streets, part fashion shops, part potholes.

Stand at night at **Bemo Corne**r, with your back to the beach, and the two faces of urban Kuta lie one on either hand. To your right is the **Night Market** and the cinema, each pure Indonesia. It is a world of luridly hand-painted film advertisements, flapping gaudily heroic canvases hung on scaffolding, and of interiors illuminated by kerosene lamps, hemmed in by the black and humid night. Prices are uniformly low, and the unmade-up roads dusty and uneven. The small restaurants of the Night Market have adapted themselves to the needs of the tourists, but hardly the cinema. Here seat prices are nominal, Rp250 and 350, and the seats wooden. The unmarried young stand outside or sit astride their motorbikes in the scruffy forecourt, listening to the relayed sound track. You could be anywhere in the archipelago.

But go a few hundred meters in the other direction, to the left from Bemo Cor-

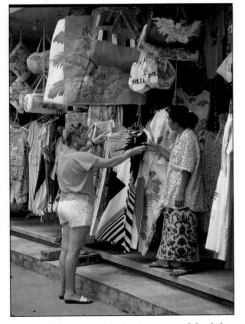

ner, and there is the flashing world of the tourists' discos and bars, Peanuts, Spotlight, and the rest, and the bars clustered around Peanuts that attempt to out do each other with amplified noise. Entrance tends to be free for tourists, but for Indonesians only if they can be seen to be bringing in a tourist with them. A tourist, it is assumed, can be guaranteed to pay for his entrance with drinks bought at the bar. It is astonishing so few locals complain of

feeling second-rate citizens in their own land.

LETHAL RIPS

There is only one setback to Kuta Beach, but it's one that could prove very serious. Hundreds of thousands of people swim safely at Kuta every year, but the fact remains that at certain points along the beach currents pull out seawards from the shore. Their strength varies according to the size of the surf and the phases of the moon. These danger areas are well known to the Kuta Surf Rescue teams, and every day safe-bathing areas are marked and watched all along the beach.

The problem is that the best surfing areas are exactly those areas where the currents are dangerous. Indeed, surfing is not permitted inside the designated safe-bathing areas. Experienced surfers are likely to be aware of the problem, and be able to deal with it should they begin to be pulled against their will away from shore. But even they have been known to misjudge the force of these "rips" on particular days.

The real danger lies in novices leaving the safe areas and trying their hand unsupervised in the surfing areas. The present writer did just that on his first day in Bali and was swept out way beyond the area in which the waves broke. He owes his life to the prompt intervention of the Surf Rescue, who noticed him even though he was far from the flagged area they are watching.

A book containing the names of those rescued can be inspected at the Badung Tourist Office in Denpasar.

The **Kuta Surf Rescue** service is run by the Badung Government Tourist Office in Denpasar. It maintains four stations along the beach, at Kuta, Half-Legian, Legian and at the Kuta Palace Hotel. In addition, the Bali Oberoi pays for a private service. Officially known as the Badung Surf Life Saving Bali, the service was set up in 1972 in response to the increased use of Kuta Beach for surfing and the number of lives being lost there.

There are 23 men employed by the service. They are on duty every day of the year, with the one exception of the Balinese New Year, Nyepi, when no one is allowed on the beach anyway. Their hours are 6 am to 6 pm.

The service operates with additional help from their counterparts at Cottesloe Beach, Perth, Western Australia from whom advice and materials have come over the years.

Remember — if you are in danger, try not to panic and raise one hand high above your head. This is the international distress signal and is what the Surf Rescue are looking for. If you do swim, swim sideways, out of the current, not against it.

KUTA'S HISTORY

It was probably here that Gajah Mada invaded from Java in the fourteenth century with his Majapahit forces. In 1580 the Englishman Sir Francis Drake may have called in for provisions. In 1597 a small Dutch expedition of three ships under Cornelius

de Houtman dropped anchor off Kuta and a party was landed. Later, the ships sailed round to the better anchorage off Padangbai, with the added purpose of being near the court of the Dewa Agung, the most powerful of Bali's chiefs, and his court at Gelgel, near Klungkung.

In the succeeding centuries Bali became a source of slaves, sold to Java but also as far afield as Mauritius. Kuta (encompassing also the anchorages nearby on the east coast) was the center for that trade.

But Kuta had always been to some extent disreputable, an area where vagabonds congregated and foreigners were allowed to settle. Parallels with its modern character needn't be emphasized.

WHERE TO STAY

There is so much accommodation in Kuta and Legian it is only feasible to mention some of the less inexpensive places that intending visitors might want to contact to make advance reservations. The small *losmen* which are a specialty of the resort can only really be selected after inspection on the ground.

Beginning in the south, **Pertamina Cottages** (℄ 51161; fax 52030; 274 rooms; rates: expensive) was constructed initially for the benefit of executives of the Indonesian state oil company, whose name it still bears, but financial problems in the industry necessitated its being sold off and now it functions as a hotel. Gough Whitlam once wrote in its VIP visitors' book: "If there be a Paradise on Earth, this is it," but its heyday is now past.

More attractive is the new **Holiday Inn Bali Hai** (℄ 53487; fax 52527; 187 rooms; rates: average and above), comfortable yet with a Balinese ambiance, and the large **Kartika Plaza** (℄ 51067; fax 52475; 386 rooms; rates: average and above). Both are on the sea, though a ten minute's walk from the best part of the beach.

Once you arrive at Jalan Bakungsari, running at right angles to the sea and joining the beach at a large cheap clothes market, you are in the thick of things. Progressing inland, and all on the right of the road, you have **Agung Beach Bungalows**

Balinese life is by no means all temple ritual.
TOP: A seller of very untraditional masks,
Denpasar. BELOW: Massage on Kuta beach. Note
the numbered sun hats — all masseurs have to
obtain a licence. Half an hours's massage will cost
something under one US dollar.

(℃ 51263; fax 53752; 70 rooms; rates: moderate), the **Kuta Beach Club** (℃ 51261; fax 52896; 96 rooms; rates: average and above) and the **Ramayana Seaside Cottages** (℃ 51864; fax 51866; rates: moderate). All have bungalow-style rooms and are within three minutes' walk of the beach.

Particularly good value is the **Kuta Village Inn** (℃ 51095; fax 53051; rates: moderate), tucked away down a narrow lane, or gang, a little further along the road on the same side. The welcome is very friendly, and special arrangements can often be made after discussion with the management. There is a choice of rooms, some air-conditioned, some with ceiling fan, and prices vary accordingly.

On the next road north, Jalan Pantal Kuta, stands the **Natour Kuta Beach** (℃ 51361; fax 51362; 138 rooms; rates: average and above), two hundred meters south of the site of the hotel with the same name that was Kuta's first hostelry back in the thirties. There's a Garuda office in the lobby, and Japanese dishes in the restaurant. Also on the same street is the very reasonable **Ida Beach Inn Bungalows** (℃ 51205; fax 51934; 64 rooms; rates: moderate).

Tucked away along Poppies Lane and just past the restaurant are the cottages of the same name, **Poppies Cottages** (℃ 51059; fax 52364; 20 rooms; rates: moderate). This famous and very popular place has thatched bungalow rooms in a garden setting on the standard Kuta, indeed Balinese, pattern. Self-catering facilities, and baby-sitters, can be made available.

Among the places on Jalan Legian are the **Restu-Bali Hotel** (℃ 51251; fax 51252), the **Mastapa Garden Cottages** (℃ 51660; fax 51099; 40 rooms) and **Fourteen Roses** (℃ 51156; fax 51835; 90 rooms), all moderately priced.

Back on the beach itself, and still continuing north, there is the **Legian Beach Hotel** (℃ 51711; fax 51715; 190 rooms; rates: average and above). This stands at the end of the road at right angles to the beach known as Jalan Melasti. Parallel to this, and the next lane north, is Jalan Padma, where the **Bali Mandira Cottages** (℃ 51381; fax 52377; 120 rooms; rates: average and above) are located.

North again, and again right on the beach, is the **Kuta Palace Hotel** (℃ 51433; fax 52074; 281 rooms; rates: average and above) while last of all, 6 km (4 miles) north of the airport, is the **Bali Oberoi** (℃ 51061; fax 52791; 75 rooms; rates: expensive). More expensive than anywhere at Nusa Dua, the Bali Oberoi was, like Pertamina Cottages, built as an executive haven. It is one of the truly special places to stay in Bali — private, intimate and well-managed. It was not always grand, however; in the years immediately prior to 1978 it was semi-derelict and a hippie haven of international standing. Life there now is probably a good deal less exciting, but immeasurably more discreet.

Kuta is famous for its inexpensive accommodation, and it really is possible to stay within minutes of this incomparably fine beach for something in the region of US$4.00 a day. The best *losmen* consist of the simplest possible rooms set around a lush Balinese garden, probably with a shrine in the middle. Inspecting them is half the pleasure, though it's always hard telling the owner that you've decided to stay somewhere else. Nevertheless, you'll need somewhere to stay that first day while you look around, and you could do a lot worse than opt for the **Puspa Beach Inn** (℃ 51988; 8 rooms; rates: inexpensive) a few meters down a gang off Bakungsari Street. As at most losmen, breakfast is included in the low price.

WHERE TO EAT

The restaurants in Kuta are as varied as the accommodation. Prices, however, tend to be competitive, with the more expensive places confined to the classier hotels. The variety in Kuta's eateries lies not in their prices but in their cuisines.

You can eat Japanese, Mexican, German, Chinese — the only problem is actually getting Balinese food, but even that is possible.

Once you've been to **Made's Warung** on Jalan Pantai Kuta you may well decide you never want to try anywhere else. The range of food is vast, from strawberries to roast beef and encompassing Indonesian and

Chinese specialties on the way. The menu overflows onto the very walls, and the atmosphere is half Paris and half Amsterdam. Both shabby and chic, it is at one and the same time *the* fashionable meeting-place and a very congenial hidey-hole at any time of day. A couple of glasses of *arak madu* (palm spirit with orange juice and honey) have seen many a lunch extended into the mid-afternoon, with the patrons finally managing to stumble the short distance along the road and collapse on the beach just in time for the sunset.

A few yards down the narrow lane immediately to the left of Made's lies a very fine new establishment, **Un's**, named after the Swiss owner's wife. Set in a beautiful courtyard with flowering trees, it is deservedly popular at dinnertime.

Poppies on Poppies Lane is an old favorite now become chic; but the food remains excellent, and the restaurant is so popular that tourists come there from Sanur and Nusa Dua and it is advisable to book during July and August.

TJ's, down Poppies Lane, is a Mexican restaurant with giant bamboo settees for pre-dinner drinks and appetizers. In addition to the usual fare — *tacos, tostadas, enchiladas*, etc. — there are excellent salads and, yes, roast potatoes. Fine food in well-designed and comfortable surroundings.

Many establishments go in for a vigorous ambiance — **Glory** on Jalan Legian, for example, with its Outback Brekkies, 1.6 liter jugs of Harvey Wallbanger and "Satisfaction or No Charge" guarantees. A Balinese "as much as you can eat" Sunday lunch seems the sort of thing you could only dream about after all those Wallbangers.

The **Bali Indah Seafood** restaurant, opposite the Casablanca bar on Jalan Bunisari, offers excellent Chinese food in down-to-earth surroundings. The spicy Sichuan dishes are especially fine.

Northerners who long for potatoes and home-made sausages will find the land of their heart's desire at the **Swiss Restaurant** (☏ 51735), on Jalan Pura Bagus Taruna. *Bratwurst, wiener kartoffelsalat* and *apfelstrudel* rub shoulders with *fondue bourguignonne*

and the Balinese buffets on Thursdays and Saturdays. The owner also runs the **Swiss Pub** on Jalan Legian, a good jazz venue, and in addition is the Swiss Consul.

At **The Bounty**, built on three stories like a Spanish galleon, food and videos combine to draw the crowds from breakfast-time to late into the night, while German food can be found at **Mama's**. Both places are on Jalan Legian.

Double Six may be a little hard to find but its style and live entertainment make the effort worthwhile. Take the lane known

as Jalan Enam-Enam (which means Six Six anyway), the second lane running from Jalan Legian to the sea north of Jalan Padma. The menu features Italian pastas with seafood and good salads as well. On nights when there is a show, a special buffet dinner is laid out.

Wayan's Tavern (☏ 51578) on Jalan Bunisari offers good espresso coffee, while **Dayu 1** (☏ 51498), round the corner on Jalan Bakungsari, offers breakfasts at any time of day and inexpensive, wholesome food prepared in a clean and visible kitchen.

The Green House (☏ 51193) on Jalan Pantai Kuta offers Chinese and European dishes, plus Balinese dance shows. Free transport is available from hotels in the

---

The best eating in Kuta combines quality with informality, amiability with economy, and all under a traditional Balinese roof. The variety of cuisines is enormous, and the relaxed joviality of many establishments is a joy.

Kuta and Legian areas, as it is to **Paul Nyoman's Bar and Restaurant/Pizzeria** on Jalan Legian, where the food is served in a luxuriant garden setting.

If you want to eat with your toes actually in the sand, then head for the **Batu Karang Beach Bar and Restaurant**. And lastly, for very cheap but often excellent food, try **Depot Kuta** (℅ 51155) in Kuta's Night Market. There are several very inexpensive restaurants and food stalls in this area, but this one, specializing in Chinese food, is among the best.

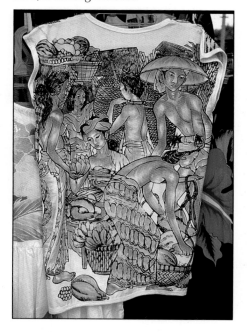

DISCO FEVER

Kuta's nightlife is both raucous and extensive. Buses of pub crawlers in full voice bump down Jalan Bakungsari on set nights of the week (well advertised in leaflets handed out on the beach), and certain discos cooperate to ensure there's never a night without a party.

At **Casablanca** on Jalan Bunisari the entertainment begins early and consists of drinking competitions interspersed with rock 'n' roll videos. Six minutes' walk along Jalan Legian, on the left, is the **SC Club**, where a giant video screen has enabled them to do away with the drinking compe-

titions. Both of these bars tend to be busiest before the discos get under way at about 11:30 pm, as is **Goa** at the northern end of Jalan Legian, a very fashionable venue for drinks, sushi and being seen generally, but a pleasant enough place for all that.

Kuta's biggest disco is **Peanuts** ("T-shirts, singlets, shorts, thongs, BLOODY WELCOME MATE!"). Clustered around its entrance are several other dance-floors open to the street where crazed revellers move to a variety of intermingling beats.

Rather more exclusive, and operating fixed entrance charges, are **Chez Gado Gado**, on the sea some way north of Legian, and **Double Six**. See the section on Kuta's restaurants above for instructions on how to get to Double Six; to get to Gado Gado you really need to take a taxi as it's several kilometers and at the end of a long lane.

Bruna's, on the Kuta seafront takes over on Sunday nights. And in addition, **Cafe Latino** is very popular. It's situated a couple of miles out of Kuta on the road to Nusa Dua and combines the functions of Italian restaurant and alfresco night spot.

SHOPPING

Kuta is an excellent place for shopping, combining, in the best places, quality and cheapness. There are some good clothes shops on Jalan Bunisari, and some beautiful shirts and T-shirts can be seen at **Mr T-shirt** on Jalan Pantai Kuta, as can they at **Tops** right on Bemo Corner.

But the truth is that there is a huge choice for shoppers in Kuta generally, particularly of clothes and leather goods. Visitors staying in up-market hotels in Nusa Dua and Sanur invariably come to Kuta on shopping sprees, and shops selling good quality goods are plentiful, mixed in with those offering tourist souvenirs. Jalan Pantai Kuta, Poppies Lane and the Kuta end of Jalan Legian are the best places to start looking.

The trade in cheap cassettes is not what it was before Indonesia agreed to comply with international copyright. Even so, at Rp 7,000 a foreign tape (those by Indonesian artists are cheaper) there is still a saving over prices in Australia and Europe, and there are a dozen shops in Kuta selling nothing else. Many people spend hours out of the sun listening to music in such places. Advice, and a wide selection of titles, can be had at, for instance, **Kul-Kul** on Jalan Bakungsari, the street where most of these shops are situated.

There are several bookshops specializing in holiday reading. Particularly recommended, both for the range and quality of its stock, is the **Kertai Bookshop** on Jalan Pantai Kuta, on the left as you walk toward the beach. New and secondhand books are

cheapest way of getting around, other than on the back of one of the ever-ready motorbikes, or, during the day, in a *bemo*.

Advice can be had from the **Government Tourism Information Center** (℡ 51660) midway along Jalan Legian.

SOUTH BALI: TANAH LOT TO UBUD

This area of Bali in many ways contains the island's essence. Here is the intense rice

available and can be traded in at half price when you've finished with them.

For antiques, **East West** and **Auang's** each offer a wide selection, including gold and silver jewelry.

There are many paintings on sale in Kuta, but it's better to buy such things in Ubud. but a mere hour's drive away.

Lastly, there is an impressive antique shop combined with an Italian restaurant called Warisan in Seminyak, not far from the Oberoi.

TRANSPORT AND ADVICE

Kuta now has blue and yellow metered **taxis**. With flagfall at Rp800, these provide the

cultivation on the banks of the fast-flowing rivers that rush down from the mountains, cutting themselves earthy gorges as they do so and providing for the irrigation that has always been the basis of the island's prosperity. This abundant water supply, and the immensely fertile volcanic soils that it feeds, is the key to Bali's ceaseless rice production, which continues regardless of season, so that the rainy season is as much an inconvenience as a blessing. The great lakes in the volcanic calderas ensure

Every Balinese is an artist, or so the early visitors to the island claimed. Perhaps the truth is that all people everywhere are. OPPOSITE: A hand-painted T-shirt. ABOVE: Work is displayed and admired in a fashionable boutique in Kuta.

an endless supply, and this in turn guarantees food production.

Famine, so common elsewhere in Asia, is in Bali only the product of political upheaval or volcanic eruption. Thanks to the relatively new "miracle" rice, three crops a year are now normal, and all stages of growth can often be seen in adjacent fields, providing the different tones of yellow and green that have so delighted painters.

And, of course, it is this agricultural abundance that has allowed Bali to develop its arts. Leisure time has never been in short supply, and with carving, painting and metalwork all originally dedicated to a religion that looked up to the hills from where the abundance came, it can seem as if the whole formed a self-contained, beautiful and life-enhancing system. And so many of the island's first visitors saw it.

The area of which Ubud is generally considered the center is the heart of all this. East Bali is lush too, but the plains are less extensive, there are many subsidiary ridges of hills, and the region is subject too to earthquakes. North Bali is a mere coastal strip. Bali south of Denpasar, now so prosperous on account of tourism, was not so long ago seen as a more or less arid waste. And West Bali has always been considered a rocky, waterless and infertile wilderness.

For the purposes of this guide, the central southern area will be considered as running from Tanah Lot in the west to Bangli in the east, with Ubud as its center.

TANAH LOT

This celebrated but overrated site consists of a small temple perched on a rocky islet some one hundred meters out from the coast. Except at high tide you can walk across over the rocks, but you will not be allowed up into the temple — it's locked except at festival times. But most people have little desire to go there; what they want to do is photograph it from the shore, preferably against the backdrop of a sunset.

There are essentially three places from which this picturesque if slightly twee ensemble can be captured on film: from down in the cove itself, from along the low cliff

where the row of small restaurants is situated, and from the headland on the right. From this last position a natural arch in the rocks to the north can also be taken, with Mount Batur in the background.

A Holy Snake

Tanah Lot has little to keep you for more than a very brief visit. You can, while down in the cove, see the supposedly "holy snake" or guardian of the temple, which lies conveniently coiled on a ledge in a small cave. Boys will illuminate it for you with a small flashlight and collect a donation for the service.

The temple itself has five small thatched shrines and is thought to date from the sixteenth century when the priest Danghy-

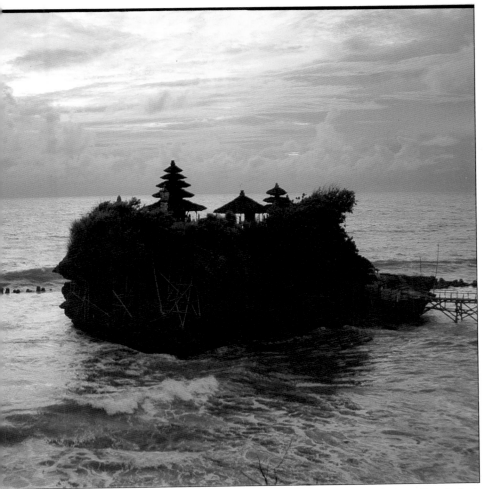

ang Nirartha crossed over to Bali from Java floating on a leaf. He instructed several temples to be built, and Tanah Lot is said to be one of these, as is the far more spectacular temple at Ulu Watu.

Entrance to the beach area adjacent to the temple is Rp200. You will be asked to pay an additional donation but there's no need to do so.

Tanah Lot is 12 km (7½ miles) from Kediri on the main road from Denpasar to Tabanan. Kediri is 5 km (3⅛ miles) beyond **Kapal**, the village where carved architectural details are produced, seemingly for the whole of Bali.

It's easy to get to Tanah Lot by *bemo*, though most people arrive on organized tours. Bemo rates are: Denpasar (Ubung)

to Kediri, Rp450; Kediri to Tanah Lot, Rp300.

MENGWI

Taman Ayun, the Water Temple at Mengwi, is a very attractive, peaceful place. Built on rising grass slopes and partly surrounded by a wide moat, it is spacious and almost trim in a way that is not very characteristic of Balinese temples. As if to establish this garden-like quality, there is a pool with a fountain in it on the left as you enter the first compound.

Tanah Lot, attractively seen in near-monochrome. The coach-loads of photographers arriving to catch the temple outlined against the sunset have rendered that particular image one of modern Asia's banalities.

In the second compound, in the bottom left-hand corner, is a small tower that can be climbed; the top provides a good view-point of the temple and its watery sur-rounds. Immediately below, gnarled fran-gipani trees exhibit their fabulous blos-soms.

The last, or inner, court contains ten very fine *meru*, the tall tiered towers thatched in black *ijuk*, a fiber derived from the sago palm. The number of tiers is always un-even, as with the tiers on cremation towers. Here the tallest have 11.

The inner court also contains a fine stone *padmasana*, in effect a giant and highly ornate chair on which it is hoped the un-seen supreme god will deign to sit on days of high festival.The back of the chair is oriented toward Agung. Also notable is an ornate brick and stone shrine with a thatched roof on the left. At the corner of each base is a carving of Garuda attacking Naga. The entire inner court is surrounded by a miniature walled moat that echoes the great moat that nearly encircles the temple as a whole.

To the left of the upper part of Taman Ayun is a lush, overgrown area, abandoned to nature and silent except for the chirping of insects. It's a place for the poetic mo-ment, and for thoughts such as that some-where, somehow it may be possible to be happy. With its spaciousness and lily-cov-ered waters, Taman Ayun is itself naturally host to such thoughts.

More mundanely, on the far side of the outer moat overlooking the temple, there is the **Water Garden Restaurant** (rates: moderate) where straightforward Indone-sian and Chinese dishes are available. Its real attraction is its location. It boasts two telephone numbers — 4318 and 6863 — but these are in fact both for the "head office" in Denpasar.

SANGEH

An exceptionally pleasant winding coun-try road links Mengwi and the Monkey Forest at Sangeh, 9 km (5⅝ miles) away. Take the road on which the Water Temple stands, turning left as you leave the pre-cinct. Turn left after approximately 5 km

(3⅛ miles), then left again after a further 2 km (1¼ miles). The forest is then on your left, opposite a car park.

Sangeh consists of some 10 hectares (24 acres) of *pala* trees in the middle of which is a temple. It is in fact a sacred wood. About a thousand monkeys are said to in-habit the area, and they too are "sacred."

There are stories of coach loads of tour-ists overwhelming Sangeh from morning till night, a horror only exceeded by the bands of thieving monkeys that leap on you at the least rustle of a packet of pea-nuts. A visit at about 4 pm, however, makes it possible to appreciate the real beauty of the place.

The trees are tall and symmetrical, some reaching to a height of 50 m (164 ft) with no side branches. The place is scented by the five-petaled flowers of the trees which lie scattered underfoot. The shady cool and the silence induce an air of sanctity, and the temple is simple and potent. It is dedicated to Wisnu and much visited by farmers.

Monkey Kings

There are around a thousand monkeys, or-ganized in two groups, east and west, each with its king. No monkey will cross into the other group's territory. At sunset, they re-treat up to the tops of the trees to sleep. Locals will tell you the biggest monkeys are "of course" the kings (thereby provid-ing an insight into Indonesian attitudes to politics). They also insist no dead body of an old monkey as opposed to younger ones killed accidentally has even been found.

Entrance to Sangeh is by donation (Rp200). Young men will attach them-selves to you and chat as you walk along, but by the time you are ready to leave you will realize you have in fact made use of the services of a guide, and a payment will be expected.

The statue at the entrance is of Hanu-man, the white monkey god of the *Ramay-ana* stories and the *kecak* dance.

Taman Ayun, Mengwi. The temple is especially spacious and, surrounded as it is by a wide moat, the sense of peace is remarkable. One of the temple's multi-tiered black *meru* can just be seen in the center of the photograph.

Ubud

Ubud itself doesn't have the feeling of a town — more an extended village. Its long main street, running east to west, is on the main road to nowhere, and a relaxed, yet never lethargic, ambiance pervades the place.

There are many tourists at Ubud as it's the main attraction for the sizable minority who come to Bali for art rather than for sun, sea and surf. This influx of foreigners has proved a problem in the past, but some sort of an accommodation now seems to have been reached and there are no obvious signs of local resentment. No doubt Ubud's obvious prosperity is a main part of the reason.

Ubud is the best place in Bali to see dance dramas and to buy paintings, and one of the better places to enjoy the relaxing effects of watching other people at work in the countryside.

Legong Dance

One feature of Ubud is that they do things in style there. You know from the very first strike on the gong that the performance culminating in the legong dance (every Monday at the Puri or Palace) is the real thing. The concentration of the *gamelan* as they play their introductory overture, their costumes and the beautifully painted mounts for their instruments, the setting itself — all are perfect. It's an introduction, and you settle down for the extended pleasure confident that nothing is going to be stinted. The relish with which, later in the week, the narrator begins his story in the *wayang kulit* puppet theater is almost as reassuring.

Yet all these accomplished performers are in the daytime ordinary workers in restaurants, shops or in the fields. These are genuine folk dramas, like the European medieval morality plays — you see the Monkey King or Shiva, but really it's the

Women returning from the fields near Ubud. The central area of Bali is the island's heartland, a rich alluvial rice-growing region where the many ancient monuments testify to a long history of human settlement and sophistication.

local butcher or candlestick maker. What is all this sophisticated talk, you wonder, about professionalism?

Information

Bemos from Denpasar to Ubud leave from the Kereneng terminus; the fare is Rp700.

Ubud has a market every third day, from 5 am to 3 pm.

There is a particularly helpful Tourist Office on the main street not far from the Lotus Cafe. Full details of drama perform-

ances, plus tickets, are available here. The nearby **Ary's Tourist Service Center** (☎ 95162) is a useful travel agency.

Where to Stay

There is a vast amount of accommodation available in Ubud and you can pay anything from US$4 to US$700 for it. The following is a selection.

The most expensive places to stay are situated just outside the village. The **Amandari** (☎ 95333; fax 95335; 29 suites; rates: from US$300 to US$700 a night) is at Sayan (see page 135) and is one of the most exclusive hotels on the island. Each suite has its own walled garden, and many have a private pool, yet the ambiance is relaxed and even informal.

And, not far away, the Australian-owned **Kupu Kupu Barong** (☎ 35663; fax 23172; 13 suites; rates: from US$300 a day) is another ultra-luxurious hidey-hole organized on the same principle, with a stunning view down to the river far below, and a particularly fine restaurant.

In Ubud itself, beginning from the Campuhan end, the area down by the two bridges and Murni's Warung, there is the **Hotel Tjampuhan**, Campuhan in unreformed spelling (☎ 95871; rates: average and above). This long-established bungalow hotel sits on the steep-sloping bank of the river. A path zigzags down and there are bungalows dotted around in twos at various levels. It has a tennis court and swimming pool; Walter Spies, the artist, once lived there. It's up-market but not new; however, the resulting ambiance may suit some tastes. There are phones by the beds, and the royal suite actually runs to a hot bath! The feeling is undeniable, though, that this was once a somewhat better place than it is now.

Up the hill from here, on the other side of the road, are the **Munut Bungalows** (rates: moderate). This is actually three separate establishments, two of them perched on bluffs above the road (and therefore, slightly noisy). The third, set back a little among the rice paddies, is superb and the nicest place I saw in Ubud. Paintings by the owner are everywhere and there is a *gamelan* set out and ready for action. Little bridges cross lily ponds. This delightful retreat is directly opposite **Ardjuna's Inn** (☎ 95809; rates: inexpensive), an unassuming losmen with simple, clean rooms. It's next door to the top entrance to Antonio Blanco's House (see page 134).

In the center of Ubud, close to the *puri* and the intersection with the Monkey Forest Road is **Hans Snel's Siti Bungalows** (☎ 95690; rates: average and above). A short way down a lane, this is classy, even smart, accommodation adjacent to the restaurant and cocktail bar of the same name. It may seem just a little too discreet for some, and there is no hot water on tap (though this is not something many visitors feel the need for in this climate). Back on the road, the **Puri Saraswati** (rates: moderate) offers standard bungalow rooms around a courtyard. And down the Monkey Forest Road, on the left, **Tjanderi's** (or Candri's; rates: inexpensive) is a long-established, popular staging post for overlanders. Also on the Monkey Forest Road are the up-market **Per-**

tiwiBungalows (℡ 95236; fax 95559; rates: average and above).

To find the small, friendly and very inexpensive **Rama Sita Pension**, turn down the lane that leaves the main road immediately next to the Nomad Cafe and follow it till it dips down and forms a T-junction with another road — the pension is ahead of you. For the two very quiet **Jati Homestays** (rates: moderate), follow the road known as Padang Tegal and it's some way down on the right. Lastly, **Sudharsana's Bungalows**, (rates: inexpensive), on the main street offers good value for money with straightforward accommodation.

People also, of course, come to Ubud, get to know artists, find places to stay far from the tourist trails, and live on for months virtually as part of the family. To find such places takes time, though, and to list them in a book like this would be an unwarranted intrusion.

Where to Eat

The nicest place to eat in Ubud is the **Cafe Lotus** (rates: average and above). It is almost opposite the Tourist Office, and both food and ambiance are superb. Hundreds of pink lilies stretch their necks like flamingos in the pond, and music chosen with discretion (no Vivaldi's "Four Seasons" here) plays unobtrusively. The menu the day I ate there offered (among many other delights) real wheat bread — not so easy to come by in Bali — salads with olive oil dressing, freshly made pasta with mushrooms, and strawberry tart.

Every stomach now and again insists on something it knows and preferably loves. The Lotus Cafe unashamedly provides for these moments, and the quality is outstanding. The pleasure of eating delicacies you long for but never expect to meet on this side of the world is compounded by paying a third or even a quarter of what you would pay for them in Paris, Frankfurt or Los Angeles.

The Lotus Cafe is open from 11 am to 9 pm, and closed on Mondays.

Murni's Warung (rates: moderate), down by the old suspension and modern road bridges over the river, is also a fashionable

place. It too specializes in Western food — head here for unexpected items such as muesli, bacon, corned beef and *guacamole*. It also stocks souvenirs, books on Bali, and some secondhand novels (but see the next entry for a better selection). Murni's is open from 8 am to 8 pm (hence it's a good place for breakfast) and closed on Wednesdays and selected holidays.

Also at this end of the village are the **Bridge Cafe** and the **Gria Restaurant**.

At the **Menara Restaurant** (rates: inexpensive), on the main street near the Tour-

ist Office, they don't have much idea how to prepare Western food but the ambiance can be delightful if, on a sunny morning, you happen to drop in for breakfast when the schoolchildren are rehearsing their gamelan and dance routines on a stage that is part of the restaurant. Most notable, though, is the lending library run by the proprietor — this has a very wide selection of books of all kinds in several languages. You pay Rp2,000 deposit and then Rp200 per volume. It provides a service unparalleled in Ubud. For a better breakfast, though, try **Ary's Warung** nearby.

The **Nomad Wine Bar and Restaurant** (rates: moderate), further down the main street in the direction of Denpasar, is a very pleasant place, open from 8 am to 10 pm. There's live music at night and a relaxed

---

Ubud. OPPOSITE: The lotuses that give their name to the village's most delectable eating place.
ABOVE: Deer-like Balinese cattle being taken for a walk.

ambiance prevails. The owner also offers a guide service with car.

Further toward Denpasar, the **Raya Coffee House** (rates: moderate) is congenial, while close to the Jati Homestay the **Jati Restaurant** (rates: moderate) offers good Indonesian food and some Balinese specialties.

Eating cheaply is no problem in Ubud. Many of the *losmen* down the Monkey Forest Road have small restaurants attached where you can eat well for under US$2. Again, Tjanderi's (Candri's) can be recommended.

Museums

There are two important museums exhibiting Balinese paintings in Ubud. The more recently established (1982) **Museum Neka** has 13 rooms and orders its material into styles. This, therefore, is the place to go if Balinese art seems to you either all the same or a confusion of contrasting tendencies. The museum is about 1 km (⅝mile) beyond the bridge by Murni's Warung; carry straight on up the road on the other side of the river and it's on your right. Opening hours: 8 am to 4 pm; entrance fee: Rp200.

The older **Puri Lukisan Museum** (founded in 1954) is in the center of the village and contains ten rooms — seven in the main building and three in a separate gallery on the left as you arrive. Again, all styles of Balinese art are on show, though less clearly categorized than at the Neka. Nevertheless, many paintings crucial to the history of Balinese art and the changes brought about by the arrival of artists from Europe between the wars can be seen here. Times and fee as for the Neka.

More useful still, however, is the display in a separate building a short walk across a paddy field away (follow a sign labeled "Exhibition" pointing right as you come out of the main museum). Here there are a large number of pictures for sale. As they are by a wide variety of artists, and as they have fixed prices marked on the back of their labels, a wander around here can give you a very fair idea of the going rate for Balinese art, and the kind of prices you might consider reasonable should you want to negotiate with the local painters themselves in their private galleries elsewhere in the district.

An Artist's House

If museums tend to make you cross-eyed with their bewildering variety, somewhere that is all of a piece and a work of art in its own right is **Antonio Blanco's House**. Erotic illuminated poems hang beside fantasy portraits of the very lady who will probably let you in and politely take the small entrance fee, the painter's Balinese wife. You are unlikely to get to meet the venerable Filipino artist himself, but you can certainly look around his studio and gain a real sense of what Ubud and Bali once were, both for him and for the other expatriate artists who made it their home.

Quiet Evenings

Ubud evenings are exceptionally pleasant. There are performances somewhere or other every night, and as likely as not old Gusti Moleh will sell you a ticket as you wander along the main street at dusk. His *Sita Leaps into the Fire* appears in the lavishly produced volume *Paintings from the Collection of Dr Sukarno* (Peking, 1956) and he will without doubt invite you to inspect his very well-worn copy of the volume. Ubud is altogether a genial and friendly place, and if you stay at all long you'll quickly get to know a number of the local artists and characters.

Sometimes it's necessary to travel the 13 km (8⅛ miles) to Bona to see some of the dance dramas (see page 58), but transport from Ubud always goes with the ticket.

Ubud on Foot

There are some good walks around Ubud and the best way to find your way around them is to acquire the amusing little publication entitled *Bali Path Finder*, a skittishly annotated map featuring Bali as a whole on the one side of the sheet, and Ubud and environs on the other (obainable from many outlets in the village).

The sites covered in ROUND CENTRAL BALI (below) are all slightly or considerably too far from Ubud itself to be reached on foot. You can rent mountain bikes (average rate Rp5,000 a day) but the countryside around Ubud is far from flat. Motorbikes are available for around Rp15,000 a day, less if you take them for longer.

SAYAN

To find Sayan, follow the road across the bridges until, after about 5 km (3⅛ miles) you meet a left, signposted to Denpasar. Take this road for 3 km (1⅛ miles) or so,

ROUND CENTRAL BALI

The area to the east of Ubud is crowded with sites of antiquarian interest. The following pages describe the most interesting of these in the form of a round tour, but it should be noted that to do justice to all these places in the same day would be, in the Balinese climate, a near impossibility.

Leaving Ubud by way of the main street in the general direction of Denpasar, turn

watching out for a sign on the right to **Sayan Terrace Cottages** (rates: moderate). A short walk will take you to this spectacularly sited accommodation, perched on the edge of a very beautiful view. It's like a scene from any of a thousand Ubud paintings — terraces descending steeply to the Ayung River far below, people at work in the rice fields, green areas of forest modulating into blue as the eye rises to focus, on a good day, on Mount Abang in the distance. It's the same view enjoyed by the ultra-exclusive Amandari a short distance away.

The proprietor is himself, unsurprisingly, a painter, and his pictures are for sale at the small *warung* on the road.

left at the first junction, where all the Denpasar-bound traffic turns right. This road will take you to Pujung (15 km or 9⅜ miles away). This is a most attractive road, scenic in a very Balinese way, seemingly unfrequented, yet brimming with artists' workplaces and sales stalls.

Painting from life like this is not at all typical of Balinese practice. But Bali is increasingly coming under the influence of foreign customs, and the Balinese are showing themselves remarkably able to adapt while remaining, in other ways, exactly the same.

TEGALALANG

Banana-tree Carvings

On the way, you will pass through Tegalalang, a small center for the production of painted, softwood statues, usually of fruit or plants. As you drive up the road you pass small shops, each specializing in one particular form or style. When you finally reach Pujung you are in a place where, it is said, the main occupation of the populace is the manufacture of the banana-tree carvings to be seen at tourist centers all over the island.

Turn right at Pujung and descend to the bottom of the valley where, at **Sebatu**, there are some attractive public baths. From there the road climbs again, past many shops offering painted softwood carvings of all kinds, to the road junction where you bear left, after 1 km (⅝ mile), for Tampaksiring.

TIRTA EMPUL

The **Sukarno Palace** at Tampaksiring is reached up a good number of steps — it is a fifties period pile with Western carpets, Western windows and international-level security. It is built in two sections connected by a footbridge over a small valley.

At the foot of the steps is the important site of **Tirta Empul**, consisting of holy springs, public baths and a temple. The water emerges from the rock into a large basin, and from there into the bathing pool. The water is considered both sacred and magical, so bathing in it is a very popular pursuit. The actual temple is one of the six most important in Bali and creates an unusually vivid impression — it's recently been restored.

GUNUNG KAWI

Take the road south from Tampaksiring in the direction of Gianyar and you will shortly be at the site of the King's Tombs, or Gunung Kawi, on the left of the road.

A few meters from the car park, steps descend the side of the steep valley. If you arrive at the end of a long day or, worse still, in the heat of the early afternoon, you might be content to regard the site from above — in this case, there is a convenient

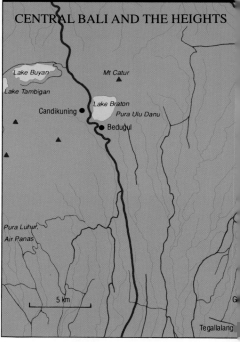

viewing point a few dozen steps from the car park. If you opt to inspect the whole thing at close quarters, descend until the path crosses the River Pakrisan by a bridge and young boys far below have set up a lucrative business diving for coins thrown from the parapet above.

The remains consist of large mausoleums, formal rectangular shapes cut into the rock and without ornamental design. There are four on your left before you cross the bridge, five ahead of you on the other side, and one last one further down the valley. There are also passages cut into the rock, rather reminiscent of war time pillboxes.

OPPOSITE: An early twentieth century drawing of the great drum of Pejeng.

The whole feeling is almost Egyptian in its formality. The monuments are thought to date from the eleventh century and to be the resting place for the ashes or bodies, of King Anak Wungsu, who reigned over Bali from AD1049 to 1077, and his wives and sons.

THE MOON OF PEJENG

Continuing further south, after another 11 km (6¼ miles) you reach Pejeng and, on the left of the road, **Pura Panataram Sasih**.

This temple, though another of the Balinese top six, is largely famous for its gigantic bronze drum, known as the Moon Face. It is more than two meters (6 ft) long, its striking end 1.6 meters (5 ft) in diameter, and it is a thousand years old, dating from the ninth century. Unfortunately, it is kept high up under a roof and consequently is not very clearly visible.

One kilometer further on, on your right, is the **Pura Kebo Edan**, or Crazy Buffalo Temple, best known for its statue of the dancing Bhima, strongman from the epic poem the *Mahabharata*, with its multiple penises.

Only a short distance further, on the other side of the road, is the **Archaeological Museum** (Museum Arkeologi) containing a variety of historical objects and fossils.

YEH PULU

Shortly after this, the road divides, turning right for Ubud and left for Gianyar. There is, however, also another, untarred road that leads off from this junction — follow this for 2 km (1¼ miles) and, after passing

through a village, you will arrive at Yeh Pulu.

This is simply a frieze about 40 m (120 ft) long, carved in the rock on one side of the path. It depicts men on horses in a hunting scene. It is strangely dynamic and forceful; there is an energy and a simplicity here that vanishes from later Balinese work where the emphasis is on poise and sublimity. These carvings at Yeh Pulu are more reminiscent of the rough but vigorous work of archaic Greek sculpture, heroic and independent of the requirements of a later orthodoxy. They are thought to date from the fourteenth century. A short walk between rice fields is necessary from where the road ends.

ELEPHANT CAVE

Back at the crossroads, take the road toward Ubud and after 1 km (⅝ mile) or so you will arrive at the popular **Goa Gajah** or Elephant Cave.

Visitors to the goa might be excused for thinking the place had received an excess of publicity. Coachloads of sightseers unload every day to stumble through a really very small cave, knock their heads against the roof in the inadequate light and

ing figures holding bowls from which water pours. They are a testimony to past splendor and are basically in good condition; they could easily be restored.

Some fifty steps lead down from the temple compound that contains the cave and baths to a pleasant natural amphitheater where ponds and a small altar to the Buddha enhance the natural serenity of the area. As neither Buddhas nor elephants have ever been native to Bali, the site as a whole is something of a historical mystery. Various explanations have been offered as

stare at a single smallish sculpture (of Ganesa, elephant-headed son of Siwa) illuminated by an oil lamp. Yet the usual array of *warung* and souvenir stalls is assembled and a charge of Rp100, with another Rp200 for the hire of a sarong, is made as if this were one of the island's greatest splendors.

Even so, the man-made cave does date back to the eighth century, and the carving around the cave's rectangular entrance is indeed marvelous, a typically boss-eyed monster appearing to prize open the rock with his fingertips. The statue to the left of the cave entrance is of Durga, destructive mother and consort of Siwa. In front of the cave are some large baths, with six stand-

to why the cave is designated Elephant, none of them very satisfactory.

From Goa Gajah it is 5 km (3⅛ miles) back to Ubud, turning right at Teges where you meet the road coming up from Denpasar.

OPPOSITE: The great rock tombs at Gunung Kawi are mysterious in origin. Situated on the valley floor of the Pakrisan River, they are probably a thousand years old and thus testify to a formal culture on the island long before the Majapahit invasion. ABOVE: One of the stone fountains in Goa Gajah (the Elephant Cave) – "they could easily be restored."

BANGLI

Bangli is a small town (though referred to up in Penelokan as a "city") on the border of the central and eastern regions, 14 km (8¾ miles) from Gianyar. Bemo fare Gianyar-Bangli is Rp250.

The small hotel and restaurant — **Artha Sastra** (rates: inexpensive) — situated just where the bemos stop, is actually the old palace of the former king of Bangli. A photograph of the young rajah, with two attendants, hangs on the walls of the verandah where lunch is served. It was apparently taken as recently as 1950. Together with the gorgeous doorways and faded gilt mirrors, it provides a key to the atmosphere of a former world. Lewis Carroll's Alice could have slipped through a time warp and been there in a trice, you feel. Yet a glimpse into the once-great rooms reveals camping furniture, and a table with shampoo and a toothbrush.

Bangli's main temple is **Pura Kehen**. Carvings of trumpeting elephants welcome you to the flight of 38 steps leading up to a highly ornate gateway. The whole temple is built in tiers up a steep slope, and its obligatory banyan tree is vast. Otherwise there is little of interest, but the whole is austerely imposing for all that. It was the state temple of the old kingdom of Bangli.

Bangli is also the site of Bali's major psychiatric hospital, something romantic attitudes to the island would have you believe shouldn't exist. Laid out in large grounds with ornate gardens, it looks from the outside to be a fine model of progressive thought. It's not really the kind of place one visits though, and prying visitors are the last thing anyone connected with this establishment needs.

THE HEIGHTS

PENELOKAN

The mountain area is most dramatically first seen if you arrive there at **Penelokan**. The main road up to this superb vantage point is through Bangli, and nothing is seen of the country you are approaching as you ascend until you pass through a ceremonial gateway and everything is suddenly laid out before you.

Turn right here, where the road swings left having finally achieved the crater rim, and take a seat in the cafe of the **Lake View Homestay** (rates: inexpensive) and admire the serenely beautiful spectacle.

What you are actually looking at is a vast caldera, 11 km (6⅞ miles) across, the hollowed-out remains of a gigantic volcano that in prehistoric times exploded, blowing away its entire cone and leaving only the bony, saucer-shaped rim on which you're sitting. It's as if you are in the back row of a circus that's in the process of being dismantled; you are looking down at the ring unaware of the giant big-top tent that once stretched from just behind your seat to a point high above you.

Mount Batur, whose broken crest rises 1,717 m (5,633 ft) above sea level, is central to the view. Its slopes are scarred with lava-flows, and all around is a scene of lonely splendor and dramatic desolation. Magnificent though the mountain is, it is the product of several more recent and smaller eruptions and its summit is actually only 328 m (1,066 ft) higher than the outer-crater rim at Penelokan.

The volcano is not to be underestimated, however. Its last major eruption in 1926 completely destroyed the village of Batur, situated at that time on the western shore of the lake. It was never rebuilt, but its important temple was relocated up on the outer-crater rim, between Penelokan and Kintamani, and this is now the place meant by Batur Village.

To your right lies **Batur Lake**, 492 m (1600 ft) below you. It is 8 km (5 miles) long and 3 km (1⅞ miles) wide and fills almost a third of the area of the caldera.

OPPOSITE: Lake Batur. The lake lies within the crater of the volcanic Mount Batur, and the distant skyline is the crater rim.

The cliffs that fall abruptly down to the lake's eastern edge rise to their maximum height in the summit of Mount Abang, 3,153 m (10,250 ft) and in a direct line between Batur and Agung.

The right-hand (eastern) shore of the lake appears to press right up against these cliffs, but long ago some Bali Aga remnants, retreating in the face of invaders, found a flat piece of land and established the village of Trunyan, where few could be interested in following them. The village is clearly visible, a prominent patch of red in an otherwise pastel landscape played over by the changing shadows of the clouds.

At your feet the road zigzags down from Penelokan, branching right to Kedisan on the lake's edge immediately below you, and continuing across the lava flows to the hot springs of Air Panas, about halfway along the left-hand shore. It is possible to spend the night at the Penelokan, but if you have the ascent of Batur in mind you would be better advised to stay at the springs.

AIR PANAS — HOT SPRING

The road to Air Panas is good, if bumpy. The springs themselves have not been developed and consist merely of a communal bathing pool where the hot water runs into the lake. You can sit in the water at sunset in the company of fifty-odd villagers, some of them scrubbing their washing on the side. It's nicer, though, to swim in the lake itself which the waters of the spring make very warm at this point.

There are several *losmen* here, all inexpensive, and one hotel. This is the **Balai Seni Toyabungkah** (rates: moderate), the headquarters of the International Association for Art and the Future.

Founded in 1973 by the celebrated Indonesian novelist Sutan Takdir Alisjahbana (born in 1908 and author of over thirty books on philosophy, linguistics, culture and education; his novels include *Endlessly Dogged by Misfortune, The Lamp That Never Failed* and *The Girl in the Robbers' Nest*), it has been the venue for painting contests, mythic dramas and writers' conferences. The author actually lives there but is frequently away in Jakarta where he holds a professorship.

As a hotel guest you are most likely to engage with the center's artistic aims through the regular dance performances given there by a local troupe. There is also a library containing a range of books on art in several languages. Generally, though, the place isn't a hive of activity, not surprisingly when you consider its remote location. But the atmosphere is pleasant, with guitar music issuing from the stereo in the restaurant, and the setting among flower-

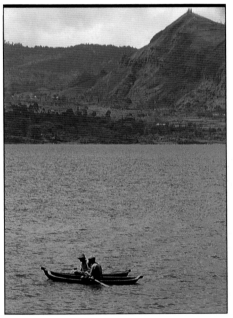

ing trees with a view down to the lake is picturesque.

The road continues beyond Air Panas to **Songan** where there is an attractively sited temple up a track to your left in the center of the village.

THE ASCENT OF BATUR

There's no need for a guide unless you plan to set off in the dark to see the sun rise; in this case you will need to start at 3:30 am and can easily find a guide by asking around at Air Panas.

An early start is advisable anyway, though, not because of the distance but because of the heat later in the day. The

Balai Seni serves breakfast from about 6:30 am.

From Air Panas, take the lane that leads toward the mountain from the center of the village. Anyone will point it out to you if you say, "*Batur — jalan jalan*" ("Batur — walking"). It curves gently round to the left until, after about 1 km (⅝ mile), you reach a temple. Pass the temple, continuing on the very clear track, and follow it as it winds across the now cindery scrubland around the base of the mountain. After crossing the second of two (usually dry) river beds, the path turns upwards, heading directly for the peak.

Next comes a steep, dusty bit where valuable assistance is provided as handholds by some small pine trees. At the top is an orange refuse bin that marks the junction of the track with another coming up from the left. From here the path crosses a level stretch and then diverges into several subsidiaries, all making for the ridge on the right. Once you have achieved this, the path becomes unified again and runs clearly ahead of you toward the summit. Views back over the lake are superb.

As you climb, Agung begins to appear behind you above the rim of the outer crater to the east.

Around the Crater Rim

After a time, the path divides, one branch carrying on straight ahead, the other leading off to the left. Take the left-hand branch for the gentler ascent. This will take you to a low point on Batur's crater rim and with any luck you will encounter local boys offering cold drinks. Considering the distance they have come and the weight they have had to carry, it's only charitable to buy one, and for only a little less than the price they ask.

From here the round-crater path rises steeply to the right. The ground is quite sandy and loose and in fact most comfortably negotiated barefoot. The wind sings

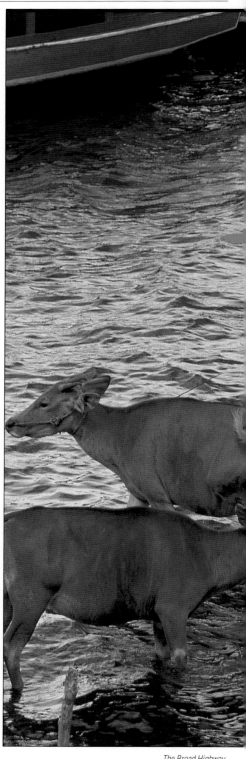

Washing cattle in Lake Batur. K'tut Tantri's book *Revolt in Paradise* contains a description of cattle being drowned as ritual sacrifices in this lake. The upland central area of the island is much cooler than the coastal region; it's frequently in cloud and suffers heavy rainfall.

in the tough grass. Make for two small pines.

Finally you arrive at the high point of the crater rim, the pinnacle that has been ahead of you most of the way up, and here there are two orange refuse bins to prove it.

You are here standing on the top of the high crest that rises so impressively on the right of the volcano when viewed from Penelokan.

The round-crater route is narrow but well trodden. It is not, however, for the

steam rises without sound, and the silence is broken only by the twitter of birds and the occasional ominous sound of a falling stone. At its center the crater is extraordinarily deep, and sheer. The steam rises not only from a vent near the bottom, but also from high up, close to the crater rim.

The descent on the route toward Kedisan begins a little way further round to the left from where you first attained the crater coming up from the springs, at the next bin in fact. The path descends steeply and unpleasantly in a continuous incline

faint-hearted. At least at one point the track crosses a very narrow ridge, with steep falls on either side and steam issuing out of the rocks just below. Anyone with a fear of heights will not need to be told to keep away.

An Eerie Silence

The crater itself is an awesome place, with steam rising silently from several clefts and giving rise to lush vegetation on the cliffs immediately above. As water is not a constituent element of the inner earth, and this is steam not smoke, the hot vapor must be caused by water percolating down from the surface and boiling on contact with the molten lava below. What is eerie is that the

to the plain. This is a common ascent route but inferior to the one from Air Panas because its steepness is unrelieved. You are rewarded on arrival at level ground by a small *warung* where you can buy soft drinks and small cakes; sometimes the *warung* is unmanned and you are invited to leave the money due in a box. (The owner is said to be a trained *leyak*, or witch,

---

OPPOSITE: Vendor at Lake Batur: there are few places on the island where tourists frequent that are free of such people, but they mean well and their wares are not infrequently good value. ABOVE: Mount Batur from the crater rim. The volcano erupted in 1917 and then again in 1926, on the second occasion destroying the ancient village of Batur on the shore of the lake.

and to be well aware when his dues have not been paid, and by whom.)

ACROSS THE LAKE

The boats leave across the lake for the Bali Aga village of Trunyan from **Kedisan**. Here the **Segara Homestay and Restaurant** (rates: inexpensive), on the right immediately before you get to the ferry terminal, will provide lunch and, if necessary, rooms.

Arranging your crossing to Trunyan can be difficult. There are official rates, advertised at an official booking office, but there are no regular ferries to take you. Instead, you have to charter a boat, and this means in practice negotiating a price with the skipper. Individuals have little alternative but to wait for a group planning to charter a boat to come along and then make arrangements to join them.

You will hear preposterous prices quoted for chartering a boat up in Penelokan, as for many other things; at the lakeside they are more reasonable, if you're determined and if you're prepared to wait. Something between Rp10,000 and 15,000 return for a group of three or four is reasonable, and this should include both a visit to the cemetery at Kuban (a short distance from Trunyan but accessible only by boat) and a visit across the lake to the hot springs if you haven't already been there.

TRUNYAN

The trip across takes around half an hour. The donations that are the theme of any visit to the Bali Aga village of Trunyan begin at the quay. Then a group of children, who must be employed fulltime on the project (despite their insistent requests for pens "for school") will attach themselves to you and lead you to the temple where you will be shown a building housing an especially large statue that you will not be allowed to see. From there, the children will lead you around some pigsties, past some hostile-looking adults (though this may be all part of the act) and back to your boat, where they will finally strip off and

offer to dive for coins. This they do with remarkable skill. As you leave, they wave and even shout goodbye, the first cheerful acts they have performed throughout the routine.

As you pull up at the little beach serving the cemetery, a reception committee of two solicits a "donation" and presents you with a register for signature. The place of the dead is on the right. The point about Trunyan is that they neither cremate nor bury their dead but lay them out to decay in the open air and be picked clean by the

forces of nature. Consequently you enter the designated territory with some trepidation. It's not clear exactly what horrors the tourist is allowed to see in periods shortly following on a death, but when I was there, there were merely seven or eight wicker tents containing in some cases a skull, more often just some bones and scraps of clothing, plus some funeral gifts such as a Sprite bottle or a few hundred rupiah coins.

A small group of skulls placed on a ledge near the entrance marks the spot where a further donation is requested. And in the same way that the donation register you sign on the beach, in common with almost all such registers in Bali, shows only previous donations of several thousands of rupiahs, so, on the same principle, any

---

Trunyan cemetery where the village dead are laid out on the surface of the earth to decompose. These skulls have been placed at the cemetery entrance to elicit donations from foreign tourists. Small contributions will be quickly removed as setting a bad example.

small notes you donate as you enter the cemetery itself have been removed, as setting a bad example, by the time you leave.

Back to Kedisan
It used to be claimed that boatmen on the lake were in the habit of stopping in the middle and demanding an increase in the fare. The existence now of an official box office seems to have curbed this custom for the most part, though simple requests for more as you approach the landing-stage back at Kedisan should be treated on their merits. The appeals may sound slightly threatening in a way they are not meant to be, as the only relevant English phrase the boatmen may know is likely to be a rather blunt-sounding "More money." Don't be taken aback, as the truth is he's only asking for a tip.

CLIMBING ABANG

Back up at Penelokan and again facing the view, you have the alternative of either going round the rim left in the direction of Kintamani and Penulisan, or right and attempting the ascent of Mount Abang.

If you decide on the latter, follow the road down as if you were going back again to Bangli, and take the second turning on the left immediately after the road begins to drop down from the ridge (the first left leads to a restaurant). It's only a few meters down, and there's a shop on the corner but no sign. This road quickly leads back onto the outer-crater rim, but now running east. After 4 km (2½ miles), the main section of the road peels off to the right and descends, eventually to Besakih. The road along the rim continues for another kilometer or so, passes a couple of *warung*, skirts to the right of a small temple, descends a hill, then turns right. There is a house nearby. From this point on you have to walk. The path is well defined but slippery, and it's about two hours to the summit, which is marked by a temple (there's another about halfway up).

BATUR AND KINTAMANI

Going west along the rim of the caldera from Penelokan, you pass two notable restaurants, the **Puri Selera** (rates: moderate) and then the **Kintamani Restaurant** (rates: average and above). As these restaurants depend largely on tourists visiting the crater rim during the day but going on elsewhere, or back to their hotels, for the evening, they are only open at lunchtimes.

The **Temple of Ulan Danu** at Batur only dates from 1926 when its predecessor down on the shore of the lake was destroyed. Like all temples in Bali, it faces the mountains, in this case the one that was responsible for its destruction. Its situation, of course, is magnificent, and to watch the gorgeously clad celebrants processing round the outside of its walls on its festival days, the wild country of mountain and lake contrastingly pale in the background, is to see something both wonderful and sad — life struggling to placate insensibility — and very much of the essence of Bali.

The best place to stay in Kintamani (virtually continuous with Batur) is several hundred meters off the road to the right. The **Puri Astina** (rates: moderate) has some rather ordinary rooms, and a few better ones commanding a view of the volcano. There is also a bar and a restaurant.

PENULISAN

After Kintamani the road continues to Penulisan and is one of the loveliest in the island, temperate in vegetation now on account of the altitude, and luxuriant on account of the heavy rainfall. It's like an English country road in summer, but forever in leaf.

The temple at Penulisan, **Pura Tegeh Koripan**, is the highest in Bali. Three hundred and thirty-three steps lead from the road up to this easily achieved view-point.

OPPOSITE: The Mother Temple at Besakih. All Balinese temples are oriented towards the mountains, and this, the island's premier place of worship, is sited right on the lower slopes of Agung, Bali's highest summit.

Few people visit the temple and there is no commercialization whatsoever. The atmosphere at the top is secluded and quiet, as mossy and crumbling as a Victorian churchyard. The air is scented from the various bushes that sprout on all sides and rather obscure the view — which is spectacular to the north, with the coast and the blue sea lying far below you almost at your feet, and extensive but less well defined to the south. The air is fresh, and this is a wonderful place to sit and think. It's almost certain no one will disturb you.

below. After the turn-off to the right it becomes steeper and potholed. The road has been tarred at some time in the past but has deteriorated and is now broken in several places. It poses no problems, though — it is just not a route for fast drivers.

The road descends along a giant spur, affording wonderful views of Agung to the left in good weather. At **Menanga**, turn left for Besakih (6 km, or 3¾ miles). After a kilometer or so of descent, the road crosses the River Yehunda across a wooden bridge, replacing one destroyed by the 1963 erup-

For all Kintamani's rather scruffy ambiance, and Penelokan's deserved reputation for excessive hustling, these crater-rim villages ending in Penulisan are remarkable places, perched on a narrow volcanic ridge with barely room for more than the one main street. They haunt the imagination when many a more pretentious settlement has long been forgotten.

BESAKIH

The road from Penelokan to Besakih begins along the route to Abang (see CLIMBING ABANG, p.148). This first section has magnificent views down to the left through the trees to the lake and volcano

tion of Agung. On the right of the road just before the bridge is the **Arca Valley Inn** (rates: inexpensive), a modern restaurant but no longer offering accommodation.

From here on the road ascends steadily toward Besakih. As you approach, a slip-road leads off uphill to the left. If you take this road you will arrive nearer the central area of the temple than if you go straight on to the official entrance, though the latter approach is the more spectacular, being a processional avenue along the temple's major alignment. Taking the left-hand route, you arrive at a car park on your left (where you must leave your car) followed by a mass of food and souvenir stalls and more permanent shops. Beyond these is the temple.

The Mother Temple of Besakih is the oldest and the largest in Bali. There are precincts for all the sects of Hinduism and for all the old Balinese kingdoms. Thousands of pilgrims visit Besakih every day of the year, and in former times the old kings made annual pilgrimages with their courts to the temple.

The temple is constructed over a mass of terraces that ascend what are in fact the lower slopes of Mount Agung, and of course this is the Mother Temple because Mount Agung is Bali's highest mountain.

also three times, and place clusters of wet rice grains on each temple and on the brow in such a way that they remain there for some time. The Brahmanic *pedanda*, or high priests, only appear for the great ceremonies, though they can regularly be seen at cremations sitting in their high lofts chanting their mantras and wafting incense to the gods.

The main temple complex, or Pura Panataran, at Besakih (there are other, subsidiary ones, especially away to the right) consists of six walled courts, each higher

The various courtyards and enclosures are connected by flights of steps, and it is these, together with the tall, multi-storied *meru* that, with Agung rising steeply immediately behind the central enclosures, make the whole prospect of Besakih so very impressive.

The day-to-day business of the temple is run by the *pemangku*, easily identifiable by their white clothes. They receive the offerings, sprinkle the pilgrims three times with holy water as they offer up flowers,

up the mountain than the last. Before you reach the first of these, there is a small walled shrine containing a seven-tiered *meru* on your right — this is the original shrine of the temple.

The wide central staircase, flanked on each side by seven rising stone platforms each carrying six carved figures, leads to the first large court. It contains the usual pavilions for offerings, *gamelan* orchestras and the like. The second court is similar but contains three ceremonial chairs sited on a high stone platform known as a *padmasana*, or world-shrine, intended for the three major manifestations of God — Siwa, Wisnu and Brahma. The other courts follow on up rather fewer steps and contain many of the

On Agung: OPPOSITE: The first rays of dawn strike the mountain. ABOVE: Struggling up the loose terrain above the tree-line in the greyness of first light.

thatched *meru* that are so very characteristic of the temple.

Under the Volcano

The Mother Temple was, not surprisingly, badly damaged at the time of Agung's 1963 eruption, but has been entirely rebuilt. The eruption occurred just as the most extensive and important of all Bali's many rituals, the once-in-a-hundred-years Eka Dasa Rudra, was about to be performed. Details of the events at that traumatic time in Balinese history can be found

THE ASCENT OF AGUNG

Besakih is a popular place from which to begin the attempt on Mount Agung — but "attempt" is the key word: it is not an easy task. Though the climb there and back can be done in a day if a very early start is made, it is better to go prepared to spend a night on the volcano.

A guide is essential as the early part of the route winds through fields, but more importantly because, if an accident were to

in Anna Mathews' *The Night of Purnama* (1965) — see BIBLIOGRAPHY for details.

The countryside around the temple is especially lovely. Mandarin oranges grow everywhere, and there is a sense of relaxed peacefulness in this cooler, wooded area overlooking the coastal plains.

As so often in Asia, the presence of items from modern life — cigarettes, radios broadcasting advertisements for hair conditioner — act as authenticating devices for religious observances. There is no trace of the idea, common in the West, that antiquity and sanctity go hand in hand, no trace of the idea that the modern is faintly vulgar. There is nothing antiquarian about the religion of the Balinese.

occur, it is vital to have someone capable of going back quickly and organizing help. It is relatively easy to find a guide in Besakih — the following took me up and can be recommended: Wayan Pasak, Dalam Puri, Besakih. He is the owner of one of the *warung* at a car park on the left of the upper (left-hand) road leading to Besakih, about 1 km (⅝ mile) before the Mother Temple. Rp15,000-20,000 is a reasonable fee.

For the climb you will need to take with you a flashlight and plenty of food and water, and to wear stout boots and, of course, a hat.

The trail ascends right through the center of the Mother Temple itself, ascending 34 steps and then turning right and going

up the broad lane between the central complex and the large one immediately to its right.

The Climb Begins

After initial meandering (not apparent until you see it in daylight) the path begins to climb. It rises, virtually straight now, up the crest of a long spur, through lush temperate forest. It's earthy underfoot, and on the steeper sections becomes slippery. Handholds are often needed, and some well-placed branches have become worn smooth by frequent use; at other times there are only thorny briars — these should not be touched. A night ascent means the temperature is reasonable and there is little problem with insects, but you should choose a date when there is a full, or fullish, moon.

First light comes shortly before 5 am, and is marked by the instantaneous eruption of bird song. This wonderful moment is followed some half hour later by sunlight appearing on the plains behind you, with the triangular shadow of the mountain dramatically across the landscape. This shadow shortens as the early morning advances and, soon after, the trail itself is sunlit.

The wooded ravines falling away precipitously on either side of you, only dimly discernible in moonlight, are now brilliantly and breathtakingly illuminated.

The Door of Agung

The Door of Agung is where the ridge of the trail joins onto the central stock of the volcano. At the point of contact there is a steep area of loose black ash where progress is difficult, but it doesn't last long. Another short ridge takes you to the Door, on the right.

At the Door of Agung, large slabs of rock overlook some broad ledges where it is possible to camp (though there is no water), and indeed various useful items such as cooking pans are often left there. There are also shrines and the remains of offerings. The rock faces themselves have been painted with the names of innumerable visitors, many of whom attempt the ascent no further than this spectacular

point. The view over southern and western Bali is extensive, though the lack of any other mountains close by makes it less than spectacular. Clouds frequently drift by beneath you.

From here to the summit is another two to three hours' climb across terrain that is partly firm, partly ash. The peak you reach is actually the highest point on the mountain, but you cannot see the crater itself from there as it lies across unstable and dangerous terrain further to the east.

The descent is hardly preferable to the

ascent. The unrelievedly steep and earthy track makes going down, grasping for dear life at trees while your feet shoot away from under you, both very tiring and agony for the toes. You'll not want to waste much time if you hope to be back in Besakih before dark (5:45 pm).

From Sebudi

If your aim is to see down into the crater of Agung, it is far better to make the ascent not from Besakih but from Sebudi. Take the road to Selat, east of Rendang, and ask from there. Again, a guide is advisable as the path is not well marked. Sebudi is a small village so it might be a good idea to fix up with a guide in advance rather than rely on someone being available whenever you happen to chance by.

Klungkung. ABOVE: Hand-painted movie posters. OPPOSITE: Part of the "floating palace", Kertha Gosa. Klungkung has the charm of an Indonesian country town little touched by the tourist influx that has innundated nearby locations.

RENDANG TO KLUNGKUNG

From Rendang, south of Besakih, a most attractive road runs east then south through Selat and Sidemen to Klungkung.

Not far out of Rendang there is a high, tapering barn-like building on the right of the road. This is for drying tobacco.

Iseh has had its share of artists and writers living there but is itself of little interest. What constitutes the attraction of this area of Bali is the countryside itself, rice terraces with forest above them and Mount Agung on the skyline. This steeply hilly countryside is reminiscent of the Massif Central of France, or mid-Wales.

At **Sidemen** there is a modern dam across the river, several new out-of-town houses, children who ask for money and the feeling that the idyll has come to an end. But the road continues down via **Sukat** through very pleasant country, until the gradient lessens and you find yourself entering the ancient provincial capital of Klungkung (see EAST BALI, below)

BEDUGUL

Fifteen kilometers (9⅜ miles) west of Kintamani and 51 km (31⅞ miles) north of Denpasar, Bedugul is a lakeside mountain resort that provides welcome relief from the heat, and especially the humidity, of the coast.

Lake Braton, together with Lakes Buyan and Tambingan, occupies what is in fact another huge caldera, comparable to Batur's, but here the northern walls have slipped seawards and it is consequently neither as distinct nor as impressive.

Ulu Danu

At Candikuning on the edge of the lake (which is in places 35 m or 115 ft deep) stands the **temple** of Ulu Danu, set in delightful gardens. Temple buildings occupy two minute offshore islets, and these, with their three- and eleven-tier meru, are, hardly surprisingly, much photographed. The temple is dedicated to the spirits that control the irrigation systems that derive their waters from the lake; there are also Buddhist and Islamic temples close by.

It is possible to be taken by rowing boat on a lake trip lasting approximately 45 minutes to see a cave and visit the **Bedugul Hotel and Restaurant** (rates: moderate). Water skiing and parasailing are on offer — contact the hotel for details. Accommodation and meals can also be had at the **Bali Handara Kosaido Country Club** (rates: average and above) which boasts a golf course.

There is a track encircling the lake, and the walk takes about three hours.

For a guide, ask at the temple for I. Ketut Sudiana, who speaks several languages.

Botanical Gardens

Half a kilometer from the lake along the road back towards Denpasar, by a flower and vegetable market, a road runs off to the right to the Botanical Gardens (admission Rp100; open daily 8 am until 4.30 pm).

The gardens consist of an open area of wooded parkland still in an early stage of development. Pathways have been established, and the clearly labeled trees, on this south-facing, upland slope, are very fine in themselves. Flowers are being added gradually.

At the moment it's a place for quiet, rather extensive walks among glades, with views up to the wooded hills, and, on a weekday at least, almost total solitude. On an island where a huge variety of tropical and subtropical plants, both native and introduced, flourish with ease, the potential here is clearly immense.

EAST BALI

KLUNGKUNG

Thirty-nine kilometers (24⅜ miles) east of Denpasar lies the former royal capital of Klungkung. It's the place where you can change *bemo*s for Besakih to the north and for Padangbai, Candi Dasa and Amlapura to the east. The fare from Denpasar to Klungkung is around Rp700.

The town has a cozy feeling to it — there is an extensive market, some good shops, one passable hotel (see WHERE TO STAY below), and a famous monument.

This last is the **Kertha Gosa**, the courthouse of the old kingdom of Klungkung. It consists of two buildings, an elegant little "floating palace" — really just a raised and much-decorated pavilion set in the middle of a wide moat and originally used as a retreat for the judges — and the actual court, raised high for all to see on your left as you enter from Jalan Untung Surapati.

Both buildings are intricately carved, and the stone animals supporting the pillars in the courthouse itself are particularly noteworthy.

Entrance is Rp500 and Rp250 for children. The monument is open from 7 am to 5 pm daily.

Where to Stay
The only hotel in Klungkung that is at all satisfactory is the **Ramayana Palace Restaurant and Hotel** at 152 Jalan Diponegoro ((Klungkung 44; rates: inexpensive). The

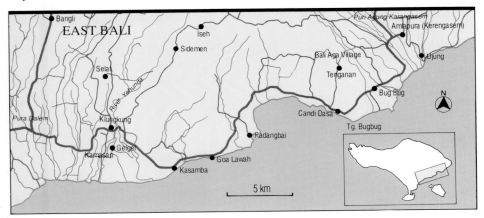

The dreadful punishments said to be reserved for sinners in another life are vividly illustrated on the roof of the little court — mothers who refused to suckle their young being forced to give the breast to a poisonous fish, confirmed bachelors being savaged by a wild boar, etc. These pictures are not in fact very old but are copies, made on asbestos some forty years ago, of the much older originals .

Everything is very delicate, not least the worn red-brick floor, and the only pity is that the whole compact complex, so restful in design, is sited so very close to Klungkung's main road intersection. But this was the whole point: the open-sided court was not only raised up high but set at the very center of the town, open, public and for all to see. Somewhere quieter among the water lilies was set aside for the judges — high priests (*pedanda*) from the Brahmana caste — to consider their judgments.

owner, Nyoman Gede, speaks excellent English, and there is a rather large temple attached, reached down a few steps from the restaurant.

Shopping
The **market**, to the right of Jalan Diponegoro, is extensive and, like most Asian markets, all over by early afternoon. By contrast, the food stalls close to the *bemo* terminus just off Jalan Gajah Mada flourish for several hours beginning at sunset. The shops, which extend along the two above-mentioned streets from the Kertha Gosa, are surprisingly sophisticated for such a relatively small place — quality batik and temple umbrellas are among the Balinese specialties that can be found.

Klungkung itself is a combination of a quiet country town and a very Oriental market. Marigolds piled by their thousands on blue tarpaulins, groups of girls skinning tiny mauve onions, *bemos* arriv-

ing from all parts, patent scorpion medicines being sold at the curbside, the harsh glare of kerosene lamps as corn cobs are toasted and yesterday's hits from Jakarta jangle out from a mobile juke box, a post-cremation *angklung* (processional *gamelan*) in the intensely hot afternoon — Klungkung may have only the one monument but it is a fascinatingly typical Balinese town, attractive in a way Denpasar no longer is, and its atmosphere little diluted by the impulse to cater to the foreign needs and tastes of tourists.

GELGEL AND KAMASAN

Directly to the south of Klungkung, leaving the town by Jalan Puputan, are the villages of Gelgel and Kamasan. Gelgel is the old, pre-eighteenth-century capital of the area and, though it was ravaged by lava in 1963, the old **Royal Temple** still stands. Pottery-making can also be seen. Kamasan is the center for a traditional style of painting. (See PAINTING in THE CULTURE OF BALI.)

THE COAST ROAD

From Klungkung, the main road east to Amlapura (almost universally known by the Balinese as Karangasem) runs down to the coast. You leave town along Jalan Diponegoro, passing the Ramayana Palace Hotel on your right, and then cross the River Unda by way of a high bridge.

During the eruption of Mount Agung in 1963, a former bridge was destroyed by the lava coming down the river valley, and a few kilometers out of Klungkung extensive lava fields can be seen to the right of the road. The lava flowed seawards in two arms, this one to the west and another, following the valleys of the rivers Buhu, Banka and Njuling, to the east. Both Amlapura, which stands on the banks of the Njuling, and Klungkung were thus lucky to escape serious damage.

After 7 km (4⅜ miles), the road runs through **Kusamba's** main street. This is the small market and fishing village from which boats leave for Nusa Penida and Nusa Lembongan. To reach the sea, fork

right at the far (or eastern) end of the village, where a building stands in the middle of the road. A lane runs straight to the beach past a mosque and a school. Ask at the last *warung* on the right about boats to the islands. Don't, however, expect to be able to leave any later than early afternoon: waves tend to build up in the Badung Strait during the day and by mid-afternoon landing on the beach at Kusamba — there is no jetty — becomes dangerous. The one-way fare in a wooden motorized *prahu* is normally Rp1,500, and the trip takes around three hours.

The crossing can also be made in rather larger boats that hold up to 25 passengers. To find these boats, go 1 km (⅝mile) along the main road in the direction of Amlapura and turn right down Jalan Pasir Putih. (There is a little sign on the left of the main road indicating the turning with the words "Dermaga Penyebrangan Kusamba 200 m"). In addition, see the NUSA PENIDA section for information on the speedboat ferry from Padangbai.

Bat Cave

A couple of kilometers east of Kusamba is the extraordinary **Goa Lawah**. It's only a relatively small opening in the limestone cliff, but it is the home of what appear to be hundreds of thousands of only semi-nocturnal bats. A temple has been built immediately in front of its entrance, and so it's necessary to pay a donation of Rp200, in return for the loan of a scarf.

It isn't really possible to enter the cave as the low roof is completely covered in bats and the floor coated in a thick layer of guano. Several shrines stand just inside the cave, also guano-crowned. But there's no need to go in to see the bats at close quarters — they crowd together over large areas of the outside walls and it is easy to get within half a meter of them. Hanging upside down in full daylight,

Goa Lawah. Because the home of so many bats has been considered sacred, a temple has been built there and throughout the day a stream of devotees arrives, many bearing offerings as in this photograph. But the temple is as interesting as the bats, and the juxtaposition of the two is nothing less than astonishing.

they twist their necks and peer at you as you approach, preparing no doubt for flight. With the massed squeaking, the crowds of kneeling devotees, the incense, the priests' prayers and the flashing of tourists' cameras, it's at one and the same time grotesque, comic and wonderful. It's situated right on the main road and no one should drive past without sparing five minutes for a quick look, however pressed you are for time, or anxious to get on to the comforts and consolations of Candi Dasa.

Salt from the Sea
Directly over the road from the bat temple, on the black-sand beach, is a primitive salt factory, where salt is procured from sea water. Under a thatched roof water drips down bamboo pipes and a solitary worker displays a bowl of gleaming salt crystals for your admiration. Nusa Penida shimmers along the horizon.

The salt-making process is as follows. Wet sand is spread out on the beach and, when partly dry, is placed in a container inside one of the huts.

Eventually a salty liquid begins to drip out, and this is transferred to long wooden troughs where the last of the water evaporates.

It's almost as interesting — natural but unexpected — as the bats.

PADANGBAI

Eighteen kilometers (11¼ miles) from Klung-kung is Padangbai, Bali's port of entry for luxury-liner passengers and the terminal for the ferry to Lombok.

Quite what the cruise customers think of the island when they are ferried in to Padangbai's single wharf — large ships cannot come alongside and moor just round

the headland in the direction of Candi Dasa — doesn't bear thinking about. The village — for that's really all it is — just consists of a single street running inland from the jetty and a few fishermen's huts. A greater contrast to the luxury of Nusa Dua or Sanur, and presumably the cruise liners, can hardly be imagined.

Yet Padangbai grows on you. It has the attraction of a busy terminal little concerned with tourists most days of the year (traders and hawkers tend to come in from outside when the cruise ships are due). The sandy beach to the east of the jetty is home to many colorful *prahu*, and the sale of the night's catch in the early morning, alongside the boats, is a colorful spectacle. Also, many of Padangbai's inhabitants are Moslems, and to stand on a hillside above the bay at sunset and hear the muezzin's song from the mosque, as a small bird orchestra circles the valley as if in harmony with the words of the Prophet, is to experience something of the Old East preserved almost intact in this strange, beautiful land.

Where to Stay
Much the nicest place to stay in Padangbai is the **Rai Beach Inn** (rates: moderate). It

of other choices, at one of which, **Johnny's** (rates: inexpensive), there is an extraordinarily amusing singing bird.

Ferries to Lombok
Ferries for Lombok leave Padangbai three times a day. The departure times are supposedly 9 am, 1:30 pm and 3 pm, but I sat and watched the 1:30 boat pulling away just before l:15, and it seems advisable to arrive, and board the ship, in plenty of time. Fares are Rp3,500 economy and Rp4,500 first-class, one way. Autombiles are Rp 45,000.

only has four rooms, but each is a self-contained two-story house built entirely of bamboo and wood, with a high arched roof and contained within a little compound. It's on the beach east of the jetty, about halfway along on the way to the headland. Just past it is the **Padangbai Beach Inn** (rates: inexpensive), a simpler affair with a nice outlook over the bay. Neither establishment has a restaurant.

Where to Eat
The best place to eat in Padangbai is **Kendedes Restaurant** (rates: inexpensive) where large portions of well-prepared Western and Indonesian food are served in a friendly atmosphere. There are a couple

... And Further Afield
Padangbai is also the place for catching a boat to other islands of the world's largest archipelago. Six ships operated by the Pelayaran Nasional Indonesia (PELNI for short) operate biweekly schedules on six different routes. Only one of these ships, the *MV Kelimutu*, calls at Padangbai, but by taking the one-day trip on this vessel, either west to Surabaya on Java, or east to

OPPOSITE LEFT: As in this example from Amlapura, erotic dalliance is in no way alien to Hindu art, while at Candi Dasa
OPPOSITE RIGHT a different aesthetic is enforced.
ABOVE : The beach at Candi Dasa is lined with small hotels along all but the stretch shown.

Ujung Pandang on Sulawesi, you can link up, one way or another, with all the other ships. The *MV Kelimutu* leaves Padangbai going east on alternate Wednesdays at noon, and at the same time every other Thursday going west to Surabaya.

A Hidden Cove
Lastly, there is an attractive little cove just round the headland on your right when you're looking out to sea. Turn right immediately after Johnny's Restaurant as you approach the wharf, and then after a couple of hundred meters turn left at the sign for **Biastugel Beach**. The white-sand beach, a ten-minute walk at most from the village and only 150 m (487 ft) wide, is a classic "all to ourselves" location. Not for long, however: a hotel is being built overlooking the tiny cove and will no doubt dominate the scene.

TENGANAN

Immediately before you arrive in Candi Dasa from the west, a road leads off left 4 km (2½ miles) to Tenganan. Motorbikes wait at the junction to take you (Rp200 to 300).

Tenganan is Bali's foremost example of the social organization of the Bali Aga (see FROM JAVA MAN TO GOLKAR, page 13). It is as friendly, tidy and above all prosperous as Trunyan, the Bali Aga village on Lake Batur, is hostile, grubby and impoverished.

The prime feature of Tenganan life is that everything is held communally and membership of the community is as a result strictly controlled. As the village is a major landowner in the area, its privileged three hundred or so inhabitants do little menial work and are free to devote their time to weaving, writing on *lontar* leaves, or simply admiring one another's fighting cocks, some of which are dyed pink. Forms of dance (the *rejang*), ritual fighting (*pandan*), instrumental music (*gamelan selunding*) and ikat cloth (*gringsing*) are found here that occur nowhere else in Bali. Full details can be found in Madi Kertonegoro's *The Spirit Journey to Bali Aga, Tenganan Pegringsingan*, a whimsical and informative

book that catches well the genial spirit of the village.

The village looks utterly unlike any other in Bali. The family compounds are arranged in long lines on either side of the north-south concourses which rise in successive terraces as they move uphill. Because the compounds each have a pavilion with an overhanging roof immediately inside the external wall, the appearance is given of a street of houses with thatched roofs in, perhaps, the west of England. At the far end is a communal meeting place, the *bale paruman desa*, while the village temple is near the entrance from the road, surrounded by frangipani trees.

The section of the village away to the right (east) is reserved for villagers who have in some way forfeited full membership of the community. It is known as **Banjar Pande**. Here small windmills (*pinengan*, meaning wings) can be seen above the houses, serving no practical purpose but constructed just for pleasure. Up the hill behind Banjar Pande is the cemetery; the Bali Aga here do not expose their dead like their cousins in Trunyan but bury them in the ground in accordance with the practice of the Indra sect of Hinduism.

Lontar
At first sight it looks as if Tenganan is all tourist shops. All the sales activity, however, is concentrated in the first street you come to; in the parallel street to the right there is none at all. All the shops are part of people's houses. In the **Indra Art Shop**, for example, you can take a coffee while the owner, I. Wayan Gelgel, inscribes a motto for you on a *lontar*. First he cuts in the words with a pointed knife, then rubs in a black oil from the burnt *kemiri* nut. He has a collection of old *lontar* books, leaves threaded on a string with bamboo

Street scene in Amlapura (Kerangasem). Few tourists venture as far as this, the easternmost town on the island. It has an undisturbed air, and its palace area is curiously inhabited, as if the descendents of royal retainers have now taken over the whole complex.

covers. The words are inscribed on one side, illustrations on the other. The texts are old stories from the *Ramayana* (see HEROES AND VILLAINS, p.50). The books are fastened shut with an old Chinese coin, Bali's first money, used now only for ceremonial purposes. The lontar leaves have been first boiled in salty rice water to strengthen and preserve them.

The craft shop of I. Nyoman K. Nurati is in the house where the Swiss writer Urs Ramseyer stayed while writing his *Art and Culture of Bali*.

CANDI DASA

Candi Dasa (pronounced *Chandi Dasa*) is a popular white-sand beach 13 km (8 miles) southwest of Amlapura. It is the only beach on this stretch of coast that has experienced any degree of tourist development, and that only comparatively recently. The name probably means Ten Tombs and refers to some ancient monuments near the village of **Bug Bug** (pronounced *Boog Boog*) 2 km (1¼ miles) to the east.

ABOVE: A wayside meditating figure.

The beach, only 1 km (⅝ mile) long, is moderately attractive, sandy at low tide, but with rough coral fragments in some places. A sea wall extends along the whole length of the frontage and as a result the beach disappears entirely at high tide. In addition, concrete groins have recently been constructed to prevent further erosion, and their rectangular patterns now dominate what's left of the shore. Together these two factors mean that whereas there is good swimming over a sandy beach bed at Candi Dasa, there is, along much of the shoreline, effectively no real beach at all.

Even so, there is considerable peace and quiet, and at a lower cost than that at, say, Sanur. Candi Dasa originated in the rage to find a quieter alternative to Kuta in the lower price bracket, and though the unspoilt ambiance of the early eighties is now long gone, the place does remain relatively tranquil, and with luck you can perfect your suntan with the minimum of interruption.

Where to Stay

The most exclusive place to stay in the area is not in Candi Dasa at all but a few minutes' drive to the west. **Amankila** (℃ 71267; fax 71266; 34 suites; rates: US$300 to $1,100 a night-this last price for a double suite) is perched on a hillside with an extraordinarily spectacular sea view across to Nusa Penida and Lombok. Each room is a self-contained villa and a road winds down to what is essentially a private beach.

In Candi Dasa proper the top-price place is the **Puri Bagus Beach Hotel** (℃ 51223; fax 52779; 50 rooms; rates: average and above). It is situated at the end of a rough track at the far east end of the beach, and though there is no beach as such, both the site and the swimming are quite good.

In the village itself it isn't difficult to inspect all the dozen or so hotels and *losmen* on foot and then make a choice. At the **Pondok Bambu Seaside Cottages** (℃ 35534; 10 rooms; rates: moderate) both the restaurant and the rooms aspire to elegance. There are two **Candidasa Beach Bungalows** —

the original one with actual fan-cooled bungalows, Number 2 with air-con rooms in two stories. The **Puri Pandan** is inexpensive, but has a classy restaurant under separate management.

Other restaurants of note are **TJ's** serving hearty western food, **Chez Lily** in the center, and **Molly's** out at the Klungkung end of the village. But there are plenty more to choose from, both hotels and restaurants, in this fast-growing miniresort.

AMLAPURA (KARANGASEM)

The Balinese usually refer to their main towns by the name of the districts, or *kabupaten*. Denpasar is Badung; Singaraja, Buleleng; and Amlapura, Karangasem. This last substitution is so common that occasionally, even when the name Amlapura is being used, it is listed in alphabetical indexes under the letter *K*. The name Amlapura was only officially adopted after the eruption of Mount Agung in 1963, and Karangasem is still the name on the lips of every *bemo* conductor touting for passengers heading east in the streets of Klungkung.

The Palace

There is only one place deserving a visit in the town, the palace, but it is somewhere that shouldn't be missed. It also contains an unassuming but unexpectedly charming place to stay.

The various *puri* are really part of one and the same complex and together originally constituted the living quarters of the family of the rajah of Karangasem. Some — the Madhura, for instance — are now virtually taken over by humbler residences that continue, however, to have the air of being within the domain of a palace.

The Puri Amsterdam, with its "floating" pavilion (ie. a pavilion set in the middle of a lake), is still largely intact, however, though unfortunately you can not go inside the main building. Karangasem was one of the old Balinese kingdoms that made an accommodation with the Dutch, and as a result the rajah's family were al-

lowed to retain their former status, at least outwardly. The portraits and other items that can be seen on the verandah of the main building suggest, in their combination of Dutch and Balinese styles, that the interior must have been a stately place indeed. Now cocks, set out in their cages, crow, and otherwise only the click of the rare tourist's camera and the rustle of the wind in the trees break the silence.

From here you can go down through the triple-tiered, red-brick gateway and across the road to inspect even more royal outhouses. Here the problem of knowing whether or not you are in someone's house or an ancient monument becomes acute. The problem is solved by acquiring some of the children who will gather around you as guides; wherever they take you, you can consider yourself "invited." The whole area is extensive, on both sides of the road, and exceptionally delightful because it is quiet, lived-in, and, with its trees and muted elegance, human and touching.

Where to Stay

The **Homestay Balakiran** (rates: inexpensive) is actually part of the Puri Madhura. It's very pretty, your reception dignified yet friendly, and, with the owner a guide too, it's a particularly attractive place to spend a night in this little-visited town.

The owner of the Balakiran can probably be persuaded to show you where you can inspect a local bird orchestra. The doves sit preening themselves in their red and blue cages in a garden overlooking the Moslim village of Nyuling. Bells and flutes of different sizes are fitted on collars under the birds' ruffs so that the instruments stand out on their chests. They seem perfectly attuned to Amlapura's general ambiance of almost sedate tranquility.

WATER PALACES

One of Amlapura's twentieth-century rajahs constructed two water palaces, one north and the other south of the town. Tirtagangga (meaning "Ganges Water"),

5 km (3⅛ miles) to the north, is the more frequently visited because it is still more or less in working order, though damaged in the 1963 eruption. You can swim in one of the two pools, eat in a cafe and even stay the night in rooms at **Restaurant Tirta-Ayu** (inexpensive), run by the same management. A small fee is charged , with another if you want to swim. But efficient and presumably clean though Tirtagangga is, it does little for the imagination — in total contrast to the other water palace, at **Ujung**.

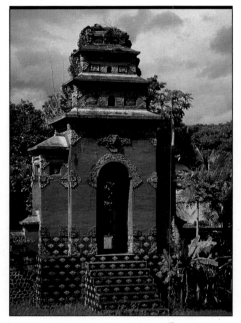

No *bemo*s run the 3 km (1⅞ miles) to Ujung and it's necessary to arrange to go by motorbike (Rp2,000 for the round trip, with additions if you stay long and keep the driver waiting, is about right). But it's well worth the effort.

The site is almost wholly in ruins, but the concept is so magnificent, and the crumbling remains now given over to agriculture so picturesque, that the whole complex leaves an indelible impression on the mind.

Ujung was built with Dutch aid in 1921 but severely damaged by volcanic activity in 1963. It was in the process of being restored (by two Australians who began work in 1974) when it was finally destroyed by an earthquake in 1979. The present descendants of the rajah have tentatively agreed with the government on a restoration program, though at the time of writing no work had yet been undertaken.

A young member of the rajah's family living on the site will act as your guide and will also show you a tattered photograph of the area taken a year before the earthquake. It's quite possible, though, that it's more evocative in its present condition.

Frangipani and palms sprout from among the fallen pillars and make artlessly elegant compositions with the grazing cattle and the one remaining dome. Above the white masonry and its flowering vegetation rise tier after tier of terraces, once gardens, topped at the skyline with further ornamental structures. A walk up steps and then away to the right will lead you to a magnificent carved head from which gushes water, against the background of the foothills of Agung.

That dereliction can have its own distinctive beauty is nowhere in Bali more evident than in the ruined water palace at Ujung.

ABOVE: A palace gateway, Amlapura.
OPOSITE: Part of the ruins of the water palace at Ujung. The original concept envisaged tiers of irrigated gardens descending to ornamental pavilions set in lakes. The remaining, structurally sound terraces can be clearly seen in this picture.

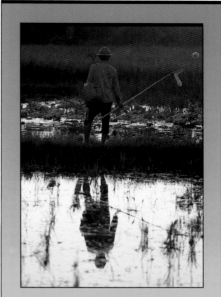

Off the
Beaten
Track

NUSA PENIDA AND NUSA LEMBONGAN

Nusa Penida lies long and gaunt along the horizon from the east Bali coast, and from Sanur and Benoa its southern cliffs present a magnificently etched spectacle in the late afternoon light. Few tourists, though, ever make it over there.

By contrast, the smaller Nusa Lembongan, a short boat trip from Penida, has recently become a rather popular venue for

NUSA PENIDA

surfers and divers. Together the two islands constitute a fine round tour, one arduous, the other restoring. They make a considerable change from "mainland" Bali.

You can get straight to Nusa Lembongan on the air-conditioned catamaran Bali Hai — it leaves from Tanjung Benoa every morning at 9:30. The fare, however, for a day-trip that includes Nusa Penida, is a hefty US$68. Alternatively, you could approach a *prahu* skipper on Sanur beach (to the left of Bali Beach Hotel) and get him to take you across. You should leave Sanur early as the trip by these small boats takes three hours and the fishermen don't like to be out on the Badung Strait after mid-afternoon because of the increased swell.

You can also, of course, cross over from Nusa Lembongan to Nusa Penida. The inhabitants of the larger island, however, and most of those from Nusa Lembongan as well, take the shorter crossing, via Kusamba or Padangbai.

Motorized *prahu* from Kusamba leave from two places on the beach about a kilometer apart (see the KUSAMBA section of EAST BALI, p. 157 for details of how to locate these departure points). Crossings both ways take place almost wholly in the mornings as the surf at Kusamba tends to get bigger as the day progresses and can make landing and departing difficult, if not dangerous. The fare is around Rp2,500 for locals and you may be able to travel for this amount too, though it is normal to charge foreigners some 50 percent more and it is not always a good idea to argue when the fare is so very low anyway. Boats leave when they are full, so how quickly you get away is entirely a matter of chance.

As the crossing takes between two and three hours, you may prefer to take the speedboat service from Padangbai. This leaves several times during the morning, beginning at around 7 am. There is one boat which is moored at Nusa Penida overnight; consequently, you wait on the beach at Padangbai until it arrives on its first trip of the day from the island. Where you wait is immediately to the left (east) of the jetty. The crossing takes forty minutes. Crossings later in the morning cannot normally be relied on and the best plan is to spend the night in Padangbai if getting there in the early morning is likely to pose difficulties.

The crossing is 14 km (8¾ miles) from Kusamba, marginally further from Padangai.

Most of the boats from Kusamba arrive on Nusa Penida at Toyapakeh, whereas the speedboat from Padangbai arrives at Buyuk, close to Sampalan, the capital. But it makes little odds which one you arrive at as there are regular bemo services along the coast road and Toyapakeh to Sampalan will take you, at most, 15 minutes.

OPPOSITE: The spectacularly precipitous south coast of Nusa Penida. That a bamboo stairway should descend these cliffs is scarcely credible.

NUSA PENIDA

A LIMESTONE ISLAND

Nusa Penida is a limestone plateau, 20 by 16 km (12½ by 10 miles) and rising to a height of 529 m (1,735 ft). Being limestone, it's rocky and dry, the rainfall sinking straight into the ground and forming underground caverns. Because of this, the island has always been poor. In the Balinese religious scheme of things it is considered malign, and in earlier times convicts from the kingdom of Klungkung were sent there.

Nevertheless, today it supports a population of around 45,000, agriculture has improved after government assistance in building cisterns to catch the rainwater, and seaweed farming—evidence of which can be seen all along the northern coast—seems very promising. A jetty recently completed at Toyapakeh should boost the economy by allowing large vessels to dock and carry away the seaweed and rock (for the construction industry) which are the island's main products.

Even so, Nusa Penida is a strange place, just as the Balinese feel it is. Foreign visitors are immediately surrounded by crowds of children — and some adults — crying *"Turis! turis!"* (tourist), and inland the roads are rough indeed. Very few people speak any English at all. Nevertheless, the cliffs on the south side of the island are worth a lot of hard traveling to see, and there are a couple of other things worth seeing in the north.

SAMPALAN

Sampalan is the main village on the island, but it has little to show other than a market. The coast road forms its main and almost only street. But it's attractive nevertheless. On a bright morning, its narrow, tree-lined shade crowded with country people is more like eastern Indonesia than anywhere on mainland Bali.

The island's only accommodation for visitors is the very satisfactory **Bungalows Pemda** (rates: inexpensive) at the east end of the village. There are five bungalows, each with two rooms.

There is no restaurant and you will have to make do with one of the several *warung* on the main street; don't expect them to be open much after 8 pm.

A CAVE

If you take the coast road on eastwards from Sampalan — and your transport will probably be a truck loaded with goods as well as passengers — you will, after about twenty minutes, reach the site of a large cave, **Goa Karangsari**. It's between Sewana and Karangsari, a couple of hundred meters up from the road on the right. Just say *"goa"* (cave) and all the passengers will tell you when you've arrived.

It isn't strictly necessary to have a guide, but a light of some sort is essential. The odds are you'll hire the two together at the *warung* where the truck will put you down. Nusa Penida has little experience of tourism, but the word has got around that foreigners are rich. Thus the few visitors who do appear are treated as manna from heaven and prices quoted can be laughably high. You will probably end up spending Rp4,000 to be shown around the cave by a guide bearing a powerful kerosene lamp. This is picturesque, but a flashlight would show you considerably more.

Entrance to the cave is through a narrow gap in the rocky hillside, but inside it's spacious, with a high roof and a level, sandy floor. It extends for some 300 m (984 ft), and at the far end you emerge on another hillside overlooking an inland valley supporting only scrub, and with few signs of habitation. About halfway through the cave you pass beneath a colony of bats, and a little further on there is a place where water drips down from the roof and a small shrine has been constructed. There are various side passages but for the most part they peter out without leading to further major features.

PEED

If you take the coast road in the other, western direction from Sampalan you will arrive after ten minutes at the celebrated, or notorious, temple at Peed (pronounced *Ped*). It stands on the right of the road in the village of the same name. It is the home of Bali's sourest deity, Ratu Gede Macaling. The word *macaling* derives from a Balinese word meaning "fang".

According to the tenets of Balinese religion, malign forces must be placated as much as benign ones worshipped, so the temple is crowded with visitors from all over Bali on its *odalan* (feastday). The place itself is large but not especially beautiful. The shrine to Ratu Gede Macaling is in an extension to the northwest of the temple.

Across Country

The real attraction of Nusa Penida is the dramatic southern coastline. Access, however, is not easy — there is no public transport here and it's necessary to hire someone to take you on a motorbike, or possibly in a four-wheel-drive overland vehicle.

A teacher, Nyoman Lindra, acts as a guide and can easily be contacted at the secondary school at Toyapakeh. He speaks several European languages and some Japanese. He will take you on his motorbike; to charter anything larger, approach the *bemo* drivers. Lindra asks Rp15,000 for the trip; a *bemo* might be Rp25,000 for the half day.

The road south branches off the coast road 2 km (1¼ miles) west of Sampalan and rises steeply and circuitously to **Klumpu**. Thus far the road is tarred and in good condition. It's after Klumpu that things get difficult. The track rises and falls over rough ground and there are frequent rocky outcrops that have to be negotiated — there are half a dozen places where a pillion rider has to get off and walk. Though generally well drained, there are patches that are slippery after rain.

Bear right at **Batumadeg**, avoiding the road left which leads via Batukandik to the east of the island. The road now is even rougher than before. On both sides are terraces of manioc, corn and occasionally tobacco, where the terrain allows them. The high hills that form the island's center rise

to the left. The whole drive, from Sampalan to Sebuluh, takes an hour and a half.

From Sebuluh, a village of thatched houses set in a hollow, it is necessary to walk. A boy can easily be found to take you and will be surprised to receive any payment. Something in the region of Rp500 should nevertheless be offered. You descend into a dry valley, and then up again to the cliff edge, a walk of twenty minutes. Monkeys play in the trees en route.

A Cliff Stairway

The path arrives at the cliff at the top of a most spectacular and terrifying cliff path. The highest point on this coast, 228 m (750 ft) above sea level, is close to here and this extraordinary aerial stairway, for that is what it is, descends almost the entire distance. It runs diagonally down across the cliff face. It is constructed of bamboo and wood, and though it makes use here and there of natural ledges in the cliff it is elsewhere supported only on trees growing out from the cliff face.

The purpose of this exposed stairway, which no one with the slightest fear of heights should even consider for a moment negotiating, is to enable the villagers of Sebuluh to get down to a place where fresh water gushes out in great profusion a few meters above sea level. In earlier times this was an invaluable source of drinking water during periods of drought. The women would ascend the horrendous route carrying giant buckets of water on their heads, while the men carried two containers apiece slung on either end of a pole. The villagers still go down every 210 days for the *odalan* of the temple down on the rocks at the sea's edge.

The best place to see the whole structure lies 15 minutes' walk to the west. You follow the track down over some terraces to where a turning-off left leads along a deep and grand valley, heavily wooded on the

OVERLEAF: Balinese *prahu* on the beach at Sanur. Crossings can be made from this beach to jungutbatu on Nusa Lembongan.

far side, and onto a spur jutting out into the sea and culminating in a small temple. From here you can see the whole extent of the stairway, the water pouring out over a large rock, and the impressive coast to the east.

There are three other such stairways on the south coast of Nusa Penida, known as **Seganing**, **Anceng** and **Swean**. But the one at Sebuluh is the longest.

It is a particular feature of the island that its supply of fresh water, otherwise in such short supply, is situated here at the inaccessible south coast rather than in the north where most of the population lives and where access is easy. But the resulting cliff routes are immensely dramatic and one of the most impressive and extraordinary things to be seen anywhere in Bali. Yet they are almost wholly unknown to travelers.

NUSA LEMBONGAN

Prahu leave Nusa Penida for Nusa Lembongan from Toyapakeh in the mornings. It is important you establish the fare on his route before leaving. They go either around Lembongan to Jungutbatu on the far side, or the shorter distance to the village known simply as **Lembongan**. The fare to Jungutbatu is Rp1,000, to Lembongan somewhat less, for locals at least. In each case the trip takes under an hour. From Lembongan it's a twenty-minute walk to Jungutbatu, and another ten minutes to the beach north of the village where most of the accommodation catering to tourists is to be found.

The brighter, more cheerful aspect of the smaller island is apparent even as you make the crossing. The colorful wooden *prahu* are remarkably stable, though the channel separating the islands is anyway very shallow. Fish dart over the coral and schoolchildren wave as you leave the clouded heights of Nusa Penida behind you.

The southern end of the island manages to attain a few meters in height. From then on it descends to the long sandy spit where the hotels and losmen are situated.

JUNGUTBATU

The beach at Jungutbatu is sandy and faces a reef offering excellent snorkeling and scuba diving. Beyond the reef there is fine surfing too. A wreck to the right, its prow rising from the water like a giant shark's fin, is a prominent feature of the seascape.

Most people come to Jungutbatu direct from Sanur (see the introduction to this section for details). At the time of writing the beach is both relatively quiet and at the same time favored by a somewhat fashionable clientele. With the sun setting center stage and the lights of Sanur's Bali Beach Hotel twinkling at night from far across the strait, it is a very pleasant and relaxing place.

The most expensive hotel here is **Wayan's Nusa Lembongan Bungalows and Restaurant** (rates: moderate). The restaurant is the only one on the beach and is excellent, serving good Western and other food in a glorious, high-roofed structure, the floor of which is the very sand of the beach itself. Bookings can be made via PO Box 37, Denpasar 800001, or by phoning the following numbers in Kuta: 51875 and 51170.

Many visitors choose to stay next door at the **Wayan Tarci Losmen** (rates: moderate). Here guests can eat an inexpensive but excellent communal meal together under the stars.

Johnny's Bungalow (rates: moderate) and the **Losmen Agung** (rates: inexpensive) provide more rooms just nearby. Most people seem to end up in the big restaurant sooner or later.

WEST BALI

THE NATIONAL PARK

Owing to its low rainfall and distance from any other water supply, West Bali has always been very thinly populated. Virtually the only significant settlements are around the coast, and the hilly, scrub-covered interior for the most part comes within the boundaries of the **West Bali National Park**. Established in 1983, it expanded an earlier but much smaller nature reserve set aside by the Dutch.

Trails link the main features of the mainland section of the park. The few who use them are usually nature lovers on the lookout for the rare species thought to be present in the area — the white starling, deerlike *banteng*, and the Balinese tiger. It is now so long since a sighting of this last was reported that it is thought to be, tragically, extinct.

within the national park, as is much of the coastal water in the area. The aim of this arrangement is to protect the very fine coral reefs around the island, the best remaining off Bali according to the experts.

Menjangan Island is the main attraction in West Bali. Both snorkeling and scuba diving are possible, but the traveling time from Denpasar (three hours in each direction) makes the day-trips advertised by agents in southern Bali a poor option.

In order to enter the national park it's necessary to have a permit. This can be obtained at any of the offices of the Directorate General of Forest Protection and Nature Conservation (PPHA). Their headquarters is at **Cekik**, 3 km (1⅞ miles) south of Gilimanuk, the terminal for the ferries from Java. The PPHA has another office south of Denpasar at Jalan Suwung 40 (PO Box 320). There is also an office at Labuhanlalang, 12 km (7½ miles) east of Cekik.

MENJANGAN ISLAND

Labuhanlalang is the site of the jetty for boats to Menjangan Island. The island is

ALONG THE COAST

The long coast road offers little interest. Some 8 km (5 miles) before Negara, coming from Tabanan, there is an attractively situated cliff-top temple with frangipani trees at **Rambutsiwi** (turn left down a short side road). And on the northern section, between Gilimanuk and Pura Pulaki (see NORTH BALI, p.95), there are hot springs at

ABOVE: The coast of West Bali is almost entirely devoid of foreign visitors. In their absence, Balinese with no way of benefitting from the lucrative tourist trade toil away to make a very meagre living from the sea.

Banyuwedang 7 km (4⅜ miles) east of Labuhanlalang.

BUFFALO RACES

Most visitors come to West Bali in September for the water-buffalo races at **Negara**. Two carts compete at a time, each pulled by two buffaloes. Because the 11½ km (7¼ mile) track isn't wide enough for overtaking, there are separate start and finish-

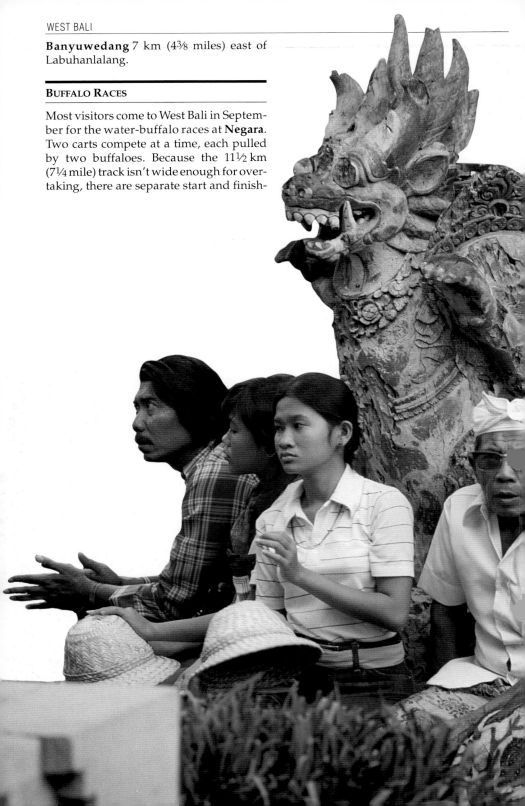

ing lines for each competitor, and the one that crosses its own finishing line first stands a good chance of being declared the winner. Nothing is for certain, however, as "style" as well as speed is taken into account by the judges.

The exact date of the races varies from year to year so consult the Badung Government Tourist Office (℡ 23399 and 23602) in Denpasar if you are in Bali at around that time.

The Balinese of all social classes have a poise and equanimity that bears little relation to their social standing or means of livelihood. (The third figure from the right at the back is the celebrated dancer Gusti Ayu Siti).

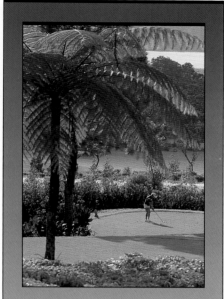

Lastly . . . the Earthly Paradise

WHEN the first Western artists arrived in the thirties, bumping over the rough roads in their early Mercedes, easels piled in the back, and sat staring at one another with a wild surmise on discovering a people who worshiped volcanoes, cremated their dead and performed dance dramas that originated in northern India, they declared Bali a paradise. What exactly did they mean? And can the culture that so excited the minds of those early visitors survive now that the island has become a tourist mecca?

What constitutes a "paradise" depends largely on who's looking at it, and more especially what he's looking for. The thirties artists were a mixed bunch, but they were all to some extent fugitives from the materialism of the Western industrialized world. They were looking for a place that had none of the vices of the West, and displayed all the virtues the West lacked. And the reason they judged Bali to be so very special was that they thought that here they'd finally found it.

INFINITY EVERYWHERE

Bali came to represent for that generation not only an idyll where the sun shone forever along palm-lined beaches, but a place where men related to each other and to the universe in ideal ways. Their relations were not commercial but brotherly, their sexual life was unspoilt by repression and guilt, they practiced art naturally and without thought of gain, and their religion harmonized with nature and reconciled the contradictions of good and evil. Above all, they lived their daily lives surrounded by a sense of the infinite in all things.

When these artists saw the Balinese at festival time dancing in their flower-laden temples under the full moon, they saw a people who possessed all the virtues their own societies lacked, who were (they believed) unaggressive, unexploitative, and were serenely and uncomplicatedly occupying their place in the natural order of things. By contrast, the people back home were aggressive, neurotic, obsessed with money, and practiced a religion that justified their violent colonialism and condemned them to lives of sexual unhappiness and industrial and commercial slavery.

The proof of it lay in the Balinese attitude to art. In the West, the artist was considered a rare talented individual set aside from his fellows, nice to have about the place but slightly odd. The arguments of the English Victorian writer William Morris that all men were artists before industrialism forced the artist onto the edge of things went largely unheeded. But here in

Bali was the very situation Morris had described. Everyone painted or carved, danced or played the *gamelan*. Here was paradise indeed!

A DARKER VERSION

There was another, and entirely different, tradition about the real nature of these islands. It didn't refer specifically to Bali, but the archipelago as a whole was seen by some not so much as a paradise but as positively malign. Along the banks of the rivers the trees rotted into the water in a seasonless torpor. Disease was everywhere. The climate was enervating and oppressive, and here the white man's virtue seemed to wither and die, leaving him a callous and exploitative brute. As for the locals, they might smile, but they were

The unaltering round of life – OPPOSITE: Fishing for shellfish near Singaraja. ABOVE: Women bearing offerings, on the beach near Goa Lawah.

both superstitious and treacherous, and when stung, quick to violence. It's a vision of the islands presented in Szekely's *Tropic Fever* and hinted at in the despairing last chapter of Brian May's *Indonesian Tragedy* (see BIBLIOGRAPHY). But Bali invariably received a better press.

THE HIPPY TRAIL

In more modern times, the tradition of Bali as a paradise was revived in the sixties for exactly the same reasons that it had been created in the thirties. The criticism of conventional Western society offered by the hippies was identical to that of their more select band of predecessors, and when they voted with their feet to condemn the industrial and commercial societies of the West, many of them ended up on Kuta Beach admiring the sunset, usually with the aid of the local psychedelic mushrooms. It was a mass movement, and their analysis may not always have been well framed, but in its essential points it coincided with that of their predecessors entirely.

THE FUTURE

If the prewar generation only began to establish a rudimentary beach culture, and the sixties travelers were the first to place Kuta on the international tourist map. Today surf, sun, sand and sea undoubtedly occupy first place among Bali's tourist attractions. How does this bode for the future of an island whose unique art and religious life, whether or not it's quite what its first modern admirers took it to be, unquestionably places it among the great cultural treasure houses of the world?

To date, Bali's culture has survived quite remarkably, and it may well be that this is not because it has been treated with discretion by tactful, highly educated visitors, but the reverse. Paradoxically, it may have survived because by so many people it has simply been ignored.

And when they have met, the spiritual has often found little difficulty cohabiting with the hedonistic. The surfer who rides the great waves at Ulu Watu 12 hours a day, drunk on Foster's and salt spume, is in a sense as singleminded and loyal to his gods as the girl who carries her offerings on her head at sunset to the village temple, each being in their own way pure.

MOMENTS OF VISION

Sometimes the meeting of the two cultures is more than fortuitous. After I was snatched from the rip current by the Surf Rescue on Kuta Beach, the head of the rescue team asked me if I'd like to attend the anniversary festival of his village temple which happened to be taking place that same evening. Of course I accepted. I knew the Balinese offered up gifts of fruit, cakes and flowers on such occasions, so I asked him what I should bring.

He stood there on the warm sand of the great bay looking out to sea, the long line of volcanoes rising smoothly in the distance. Then he turned to me and smiled.

"The gods have need of nothing," he said quietly.

At the house of Filipino artist Antonio Blanco, Ubud. There is hardly a corner of Balinese life where some indication of hope, some sign of joy can't be found.

Lastly . . . the Earthly Paradise

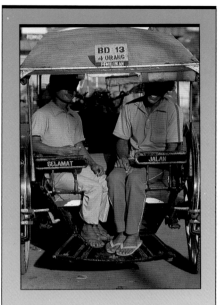

Travelers' Tips

PASSPORTS, VISAS, ETC.

Passports must be valid for six months from date of entry into Indonesia.

You do not need to acquire a visa in advance if you are a passport holder of one of the following countries: Australia (unless you're a journalist), Austria, Belgium, Brunei, Canada, Denmark, Finland, France, Greece, Hong Kong, Iceland, Ireland, Italy, Japan, Luxembourg, Malaysia, the Netherlands, New Zealand, Norway, the Philippines, Singapore, South Korea, Spain, Sweden, Switzerland, Taiwan, Thailand, the United Kingdom, the United States, West Germany and Yugoslavia.

For all the above, passports will be stamped allowing a stay of two months on arrival in Indonesia. You must, however, be in possession of a ticket out of the country (though "purchase of a ticket is also accepted"), and entry must be through one of the following:

Airports: Ambon (Pattimura), Batam (Batubesar), Biak (Fran Kaisiepo), Bali (Ngurah Rai), Jakarta (Halim/Soekarno-Hatta), Kupang (El Tari), Manado (Sam Ratulangi), Medan (Polonia), Padang (Tabing), Pekan-Baru (Simpangtiga), Pontianak (Soepadio).

Sea Ports: Bali (Benoa/Padangbai), Jakarta (Tanjung Priok), Batam (Batu Ampar), Manado (Bitung), Medan (Belawan), Ambon (Yos Soedarso), Semarang (Tanjung Mas), Surabaya (Tanjung Perak).

These visaless two-month stays can theoretically be extended for one more month, but the trouble and expense are such that almost everyone prefers to leave Indonesia and then re-enter again. This is a common practice, however, and you can fly from Bali to Singapore and back again on the same day with a minimum of fuss.

Nationals of all other countries must obtain their visas in advance; these are of various kinds and can mostly be extended at least once.

Holders of Portuguese passports are, at the time of writing, not allowed to enter Indonesia even if they have somehow or other managed to acquire a visa.

If you do need to renew a visa in Bali, the Immigration Office (Kantor Imigrasi) is at Renon Complex, Niti Mandala in Denpasar. It's open from 7 am to 1 pm Monday to Thursday, closes at 11 am Fridays, 12 noon Saturdays, and is shut on Sundays.

CUSTOMS ALLOWANCES

If you are entering Indonesia under the two month visaless arrangement, or for a conference, you may bring with you 150 cigars or 600 cigarettes or 300 grams of tobacco. If you hold a one-week visa you can bring a third of this amount, and a two-week visa, two thirds. All visitors may bring in two liters of alcoholic beverages in opened bottles, a "reasonable quantity" of perfume, and gifts up to a value of US$100. Birds, dogs, cats and monkeys are not allowed into certain parts of Indonesia of which Bali is one.

Customs officials can be difficult in Bali. Some may demand that you leave items such as videos or personal computers at the airport to be collected on departure. Strong protests, however, will usually result in the serial numbers being written in your passport instead.

DRUGS

Don't be tempted to import or use drugs in Bali. Under the Indonesian Narcotic Drugs Law of 1976, it is an offense for anyone to have knowledge of drug use and not pass it on to the police. As for actual possession, amounts are irrelevant, and it is in no way the case that having a small amount constitutes only a minor offense.

Maximum penalties are as follows: for possessing cannabis or cocaine, six years' imprisonment, with a fine of Rp10 million; for possessing "other narcotic drugs," ten years and Rp15 million. Selling or importing drugs is punishable by a 21-year sentence, or life, with the death penalty available for the second category of substances (though to date this has not been imposed in a drugs case anywhere in Indonesia).

The prison for southern Bali is at Kerobokan, just north of Kuta, and recently there were over thirty foreigners serving sentences there for drugs offenses.

There was a time when Bali was considered a paradise for psychedelic experiences. It is emphatically not so now. Visitors should neither import nor use any narcotic substances there — you may never know who told on you as informers are protected by Indonesian law from identification in court.

Be warned.

HEALTH

There are no obligatory vaccinations required for entry into Indonesia, other than for yellow fever if you have been in an infected area during the previous six days. It's a good idea, though, to consult your doctor and perhaps have an anti-tetanus vaccination anyway before leaving home.

Malaria exists all over Indonesia and, though the risk in southern Bali is small, you should nevertheless play safe and take malaria pills to cover your stay on the island. The most convenient ones have to be taken once a week, beginning before you arrive and continuing for several weeks after you leave. Get advice on the most appropriate brand as resistance to chloroquine has been reported from parts of Indonesia.

Because of the risk of hepatitis, beware of food sold from roadside stalls or carts, and drink only bottled water and soft drinks, or water that has been properly boiled.

Your main enemy is probably the sun. Get into the habit of wearing a hat, avoid sunbathing in the middle of the day, and only lie on the beach for short periods during your first few days. Suntan lotions with a high protection factor will help. Just take care, find your own tolerance levels, and don't try to look like a hardened surfer, or a Balinese, after your first afternoon.

If you do get ill, there are local health clinics known as *puskesmas*, but tourists are not expected to use them and you could find yourself being charged distinctly non-local rates for very elementary treatment. It's a better idea to go to one of the Western doctors attached to the Hyatt, Bali Beach or Nusa Dua hotels — they'll almost always see you, even though you're not a guest.

In case of serious illness or injury, it is best to leave Bali as soon as possible for treatment in Singapore or Australia. Local hospitals and clinics are not well equipped.

Mosquito bites do tend to become septic, almost as a matter of course. It's wise to carry some antibiotic ointment for use on these and other more serious cuts and abrasions.

And anyone with professional medical knowledge in Asia will want to carry with him a private medical kit for first aid or for the cases of often horrific skin disease he will inevitably encounter.

CURRENCY

You can bring unlimited amounts of foreign currency into Indonesia but only up to Rp50,000 in Indonesian money, and this latter must be declared on entry.

But there's very little reason for acquiring rupiahs before you arrive in Bali. The exchange kiosk at the airport stays open until after the last flight of the day has arrived, and rates are virtually identical to those offered by the banks and the money changers in Kuta, Sanur, etc. In addition, exchange rates for the rupiah are often not particularly advantageous outside Indonesia.

Rupiahs come in 25, 50, 100 and 500 rupiah coins, and 100, 500, 1,000, 5,000, 10,000 and 20,000 notes. The small denomination coins are very rarely seen nowadays. At the time of writing 16 rupiahs bought just US$0.01. There isn't much you can buy for that, even in Indonesia. Note that in the supermarkets you will often be given sweets (candies) instead of small change.

Money-changing facilities are found everywhere in the tourist areas of southern Bali, and they offer rates virtually identical to those given by the banks. What the banks are useful for, though, is getting money sent to you in Bali from abroad, and as safekeeping for documents and valuables.

The **Pan Indonesian Bank** (℡ 51076-8) on Jalan Legian in Kuta, close to Spotlight Disco, provides both these services. The **Eskpor-Impor Bank** at Jalan Mada 87 in Denpasar will also handle money transactions from abroad for you. Also in the Kuta area are the **Bank Central Asia** and the **Bank Data**. This last's **Card Centre** on the road out to Denpasar gives cash on all major credit cards and is much used by tourists.

It's a good idea when somebody transfers money to you from abroad for them to send you a copy of the transfer notice to an address other than the bank, just to be on the safe side.

When traveling to villages up-country, make sure you have plenty of small change as large notes can often not be changed away from the tourist areas.

At the time of writing, one US dollar bought 2,000 rupiahs.

FROM THE AIRPORT

Ngurah Rai is the official name for Denpasar airport, after the hero who led a resistance group against the Dutch in 1946. There's a statue of him at the T-junction at the end of the airport road, where you turn left for Sanur or right for Nusa Dua. The airport is often just referred to as Tuban after the village nearby.

The airport is very close to all the major resorts in southern Bali. In addition, taxis charging strictly controlled fares are always waiting to take you the short distance to your hotel.

If you're going to Kuta and really want to economize, you could catch a *bemo* (daylight hours only). Leave the international terminal through the car park, pass the domestic terminal on your right and continue on till a road leads in from the left. It's about 400 m (1312 ft). Stand at the junction and the *bemos* (blue transit vans) coming out of the side road will find you. The fare to Kuta is Rp200.

If you've any problems on arriving, try the Airport Information Desk. The attendants are particularly helpful. Ask for Mr Ketut Open: there isn't much about Bali he doesn't know.

DEPARTURE TAX

There is a Departure Tax of Rp11,000 on international and Rp5,000 on domestic flights.

ACCOMMODATION

There is every possible type of accommodation available in Bali, but the choice drops dramatically once you leave the southeast.

All the international-standard hotels are in Nusa Dua, Sanur or Kuta. There is no accommodation other than five-star hotels in Nusa Dua; a reasonable range, but nothing very cheap, in Sanur; and everything from the most expensive beach hotel on the island to rooms for US$4 a night in Kuta.

Like everything else in Indonesia, accommodation is excellent value when you're bringing in major foreign currencies, though the now usual habit of quoting rates in US dollars in the more expensive hotels fails to disguise a major hike there in recent years.

And, at the other end of the scale, a cheap room in a *losmen* or homestay will almost invariably be clean, have an overhead fan, and look out onto a central garden. It will have a cold-water shower, and breakfast (of tea or coffee with toast and fruit) will be included in the overnight price.

Once you leave this tourist belt, however, you are unlikely to have much choice as to where to spend the night.

There are *losmen* almost everywhere, and even where there are none the friendly local people will be only too eager to adjust the family arrangements in order to provide you with a room for the night and themselves with some additional income.

There are, of course, subsidiary tourist enclaves, such as at Lovina in the north and Candi Dasa in the east, where there are better-quality small hotels. In Denpasar there is one reasonable hotel, and many that are far from prepossessing. And at Ubud there is again a wide range to choose from.

The rates in the body of the text are based on the price of the average double room. Equivalents are:
Inexpensive: under Rp30,000 (US$15)
Moderate: Rp30,000-70,000 (US$15-35)
Average and above: Rp70,000-160,000 (US$35-80)
Expensive: over Rp400,000 (US$200)

Note that Bali's high seasons are July and August, and 20 December to approximately 20 January. Higher prices can be expected at these times.

RESTAURANTS

In the Kuta-Sanur area, Indonesian food approaches being a rarity. It's sometimes easier to get a Mexican, Italian or German meal than a Balinese one. You certainly never need eat non-Western food if you don't want to. In Nusa Dua, all the hotels have several restaurants offering food that could well have been prepared in New York, Paris or Rome.

Elsewhere on the island you'll have to put up with what you find. In all the places tourists frequent, attempts will be made to offer Western-style food, but these will often not amount to anything very different from the local fare. But, as with hotels, there are eating-places here and there that are both unexpected and a delight to discover.

Rates in the text are based on the price of a meal for two with one alcoholic drink apiece. But note that alcohol prices are generally at Western levels or above, and a couple more drinks can quickly double the price of any meal.
Inexpensive: under Rp10,000 (US$6)
Moderate: Rp10,000-20,000 (US$6-12)
Average and above: Rp20,000-40,000 (US$12-24)
Expensive: over Rp40,000 (US$24)

Travelers' Tips

It is important to remember that prices at the budget end of the scale are very low. It is possible to eat a simple meal for around Rp2,000 (US$1), and to find a *losmen* room for Rp4,000 (US$2) almost anywhere in Bali outside the southern tourist belt. Double these figures for these popular areas.

AIRLINE OFFICES

Most flights into and out of Denpasar are by Garuda Indonesia, even though many of

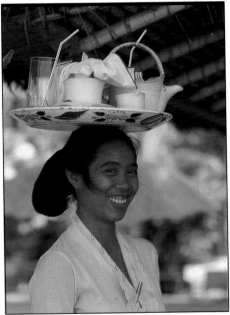

them are operated jointly with other airlines. You book with, say, Singapore Airlines but find you are on a Garuda plane at least for the last leg.

Garuda Indonesia's head office in Bali is at Jalan Melati 61, (27825 and 22788. They also maintain the following offices:
Kuta, (51176 and 51177.
Galleria, Nusa Dua (71444 and 71864
Jalan Veteran 3 in Denpasar, (33851 and 34916.

The charm of Bali is the charm of the people. There are better beaches on other islands, and less trying climates on other continents. Yet Bali has what perhaps nowhere else has in quite the same way – a wealth of dignified ease.

Nusa Dua's Galleria office also acts as a check-in center.

Other airlines are in the following locations:

Bouraq Indonesia, Jalan Jend Sudirman 19a, Denpasar, (23564.

Cathay Pacific, Bali Beach Hotel, Sanur, (88511 and 88576.

China Airlines, Bali Beach Hotel, Sanur, (87840-1 and 88511.

Continental, Bali Beach Hotel, Sanur, (87774 and 88511.

KLM, Bali Beach Hotel, Sanur, (87576, 87577 and 88511.

Korean Airlines, Bali Beach Hotel, Sanur, (89402 and 88511.

Lufthansa, Bali Beach Hotel, Sanur, (87069 and 88511.

Malaysian Airlines, Bali Beach Hotel, Sanur, (8511 ext 165.

Merpati Nusantara, Jalan Melati 57, Denpasar, (22864, 18842 and 31962.

Qantas, Bali Beach Hotel, Sanur, (88332 and 88511.

Sempati Air, Jalan Airport, Tuban, (54218-9.

Singapore Airlines, Hotel Bali Beach, Sanur, (87940 and 88511.

Thai International, Bali Beach Hotel, Sanur, (88141 and 88511.

UTA French Airlines, Bali Beach Hotel, Sanur, (88511.

TRAVEL AGENTS AND TOURS

These are a few of the many travel agents based in Bali. Tours are usually one-day round trips, taking in three or four celebrated sites and including lunch.

Carefree Bali Holiday, Jalan Bakungsari, Kuta, (28781 ext 128.

Natrabu, Jalan Kecubung, Denpasar, (25448/25449/23452/24925. Telex: 35144 NATRABU DPS.

Pacto, PO Box 52 DPS — Denpasar, Jalan Tanjung Sari, Sanur, (8247/8248/8249. Telex: 35110 PACTO BALI.

PT Genta Bali Tours, Tourist Beach Inn, Jalan Segara, Sanur, (88418 (especially for long-haul tours in Indonesia).

Tours of longer than a day are unusual, but anything can be arranged on Bali. Ex-

press an interest to one of the drivers used by your hotel, or any of the talented free-lancers waiting about at Kuta's Bemo Corner, and you will have a personalized package tour with a very special price assembled for you within the quarter hour.

OVERLAND TO JAVA

Numerous bus companies operate on the Denpasar-Surabaya route, often overnight. A good one is **Artha Mas**, with offices at Jalan Diponegoro 23 in Denpasar ((25042) and the Hotel Bali, Jalan Makam Peneleh 77 in Surabaya ((471984). The fare includes the short ferry crossing from Gilimanuk to Banyuwangi, and a free meal at one of the stops. Videos are screened on the bus during the first part of the journey.

There is no railway on Bali, but from Banyuwangi on the tip of Java a fast and modern service runs to Jakarta. The best Indonesian trains are luxurious and a pleasure to travel on, and the through express to Jakarta is one of these. Local trains are a different matter, however, though extraordinarily cheap. Information about connections to Surabaya and Yojyakarta, as well as the special train to Jakarta, can be obtained at the railway's office at Jalan Diponegoro 172 in Denpasar.

TRANSPORT

CAR RENTAL

Renting a car is one way of seeing Bali, and the Suzuki Jimny, handy for the rougher roads, is particularly popular. These and other vehicles can be rented from the following:

Avis Car Rental, Jalan Raya, Kuta, (51474.

Bali Beringin Rent Car, Jalan Raya Airport 2, (51356.

Bali Car Rental, Jalan Bypass Ngurah Rai, (8359/8550.

Bali Central Rent-a-car, Kuta Beach, (51313/51195.

Bali Happy, Jalan Raya Tuban, (51954.

Bali Purnama, Jalan Melasti, Legian, (51901/51792.

C.V. Karya Int., Utara Bali Hyatt, (8334/8521.

Europ Car, Trio Bali Int., Jalan Raya Sanur/Pandu 5, (25830/26830.

You must, of course, be in possession of an up-to-date international driver's license to drive on the island.

BEMO CULTURE

Bemos are a way of life, and one of the easiest ways of seeing something of the life of the ordinary Balinese people. It's a common occurrence to ride in these small, open-backed vans in the company of sacks of rice, chickens and even a couple of pigs.

Fares are fixed, and everyone except the tourist knows them. It isn't a bargaining situation. Nevertheless, as it seems eminently reasonable to take from a foreigner money he seems to want to throw away, larger amounts than necessary are usually accepted if you don't keep your wits about you. The best plan, if you don't know the correct fare, is to watch what the locals hand over, and to keep a stock of small coins so that you can offer the exact fare, or what you judge might well be the right fare, without leaving it up to the conductor to decide whether or not to give you any change. There are no tickets.

Nor are there timetables. The *bemo* drivers hire their vehicles on a day-to-day basis and consequently have to do their best to recoup the hire charge and make what profit they can. *Bemos* leave when they're full, rarely before. They can't be relied on running after dark, except on the Denpasar-Kuta run; in some places, such as the mountain villages of Penelokan and Kintamani, or in the country around Ubud, the last *bemos* of the day tend to leave well before five. Check on your outward journey so as not to take any chances.

You can sit in the front alongside the driver if you like; there's no extra charge (ie. it isn't "first class"). You pay the conductor (or *kernet*) as you leave for the distance you've traveled. There are no fixed stops, other than at each end of the route; when you want to get out, shout "Stopa!"

or just "Stop!" To get on, wave one down — you won't have any trouble as they're on permanent lookout for custom, with the *kernet* calling out the *bemo*'s destination to pedestrians as it passes. If you aren't sure if the *bemo* you hail is going where you want to go, just ask. No one will mind if you stopped them for nothing — they're as hungry for travelers as bees for nectar. And crowd in wherever you can: no *bemo* was ever too full to take another passenger.

You won't have been using *bemos* long before some driver suggests you charter

one. This means you decide where it goes and use it like a taxi. He's an independent operator and is under no obligation to ply any particular route. It's a good way to get to somewhere off the beaten track fast, but it won't be especially cheap, and the driver will hope you're not going to mind if he picks up extra passengers in the normal way as well. But the system has all the charm and convenience of earlier times in more "developed" countries when travel, like buying and selling, was a simple matter of an arrangement between those who needed and those willing to fulfill the need. The existence of the need made certain that someone would move in to satisfy it. *Bemos* are undoubtedly bumpy and hot, but riding in one often conveys something unavailable in air-conditioned coaches — the romance of travel.

Renting a motorbike is easy in Bali – but you do need a licence.

MOTORBIKES

An estimated ten thousand visitors a year rent motorbikes while on Bali. It's an excellent way to see the island, and especially good for getting away from the main tourist trail. Take extra care on the main roads, however, where the traffic in recent years has become very heavy.

Most people rent from **Bakor Motor**, an agency that is in effect a collective of motorbike owners. Register with them, tell them the kind of machine you require, and one plus its owner will quickly appear at your address, ready to negotiate a deal. The deal is then registered by Bakor, and you take out an insurance policy, also through the agency, for something around Rp30,000 a month. Any subsequent dispute with the owner can be settled through Bakor.

If you don't have an international driver's license, validated for motorcycle use, you will have to get a special permit to ride a motorbike in Bali. You go to the Denpasar Police Office (Bakor will take you) and undergo a test involving recognizing road signs and showing you can drive your bike around a figure-of-eight without putting a foot down on the ground.

Bakor's main office is in Kuta, with branches in Ubud and Sanur.

MEDIA

TELEVISION AND RADIO

There are two television stations in Indonesia, one state and one private (RCTI). Unfortunately television news transmissions in English are only beamed to the Jakarta area.

But twiddle the knobs of your hotel-room radio and you should find a program in English beginning at 9 pm nightly.

NEWSPAPERS

There are three English-language papers published in Jakarta, *The Indonesia Times*, *The Jakarta Post* and *The Indonesia Observer*. They are normally on sale in southern Bali from about mid-morning on the day of issue. In addition the *Bali Post* carries two pages in English.

The Indonesia Times advertises a price "in Jakarta" of Rp300, but expect to pay twice this in Bali. This increase represents air-freight costs plus the extra palms the paper's passed through. Remember, too, the boy who will probably sell you the paper depends on the difference between what you give him and what he must give his employer for his only income. Don't begrudge him the odd Rp200 — it's only ten American cents after all.

There's also an English-language news magazine published weekly. It's called *Indonesia*.

COMMUNICATIONS

TELEPHONE

The telephone used not to be one of Bali's great strengths. Subscribers told stories of "secret sharers" who occupied their line and pushed up their bill even when they were temporarily disconnected for non-payment, and you would as a matter of course have to try 20 or 30 times before getting a line.

Things are a lot better now. Even so, there are no coin boxes that work and the best tactic is to use a phone in a hotel.

Tones are as follows: ready for dialing — a continuous tone; ringing — long repeated tones; occupied — short repeated pips.

The area codes for the whole of south Bali, including Kuta, Sanur, Nusa Dua and Denpasar, is 0361. For north Bali it's 0362. The following may be useful:

Operator   100
Fire   113
Police   110
Ambulance   118, 26305
International operator   102
Time   103
International inquiries   106
Directory inquiries   108
Complaints   117

MAIL

To find the Post Office, ask for *Kantor Pos*. In Kuta, it's close to the Night Market, with a very efficient sub-office in Jalan Bakungsari close to the junction with the main Denpasar-Tuban road. In Sanur, it's on Jalan Segara. Denpasar Post Office is inconveniently placed on the road to Sanur, away from the town center.

Many people have their mail sent care of American Express. Their office is in the Bali Beach Hotel at Sanur.

As in many Asian countries, it is advisable to try to see the clerk actually cancel your stamps. Relative money values are such that the postage on a heavy letter overseas can equal a day's pay for an Indonesian worker; consequently the temptation to remove your stamps might very occasionally be irresistible. The present writer has never heard of this happening in Bali, however.

Register any important or valuable mail.

Many "postal agents" will sell stamps, accept your mail and post it for you and they are generally quite reliable.

Express is extremely cheap and should save a couple of days. At the time of writing, postal rates were as follows:

Airmail postcard
Australia and Asia Rp600
Europe Rp800
America and Africa Rp1,000

Airmail Letters up to 10g
Australia and Asia Rp800
Europe Rp1,100
America and Africa Rp1,500

Aerograms
as for airmail postcards

Parcels up to 1 kg
Australia and Asia Rp26,000
Europe Rp37,000
America and Africa Rp57,000

There is a fax office on Jalan Legian, Kuta, very close to the side street leading to Peanuts discotheque.

TIME

Bali is one hour ahead of Java, seven hours ahead of GMT, and three hours behind Australian Eastern Standard Time. It is 13 hours ahead of New York and 16 hours ahead of California.

CLOTHING

The government issues a poster detailing undesirable and preferred modes of dress. What it is saying, behind the now outmoded depiction of undesirable forms of Western dress, is that tourists should remember that this is someone else's country and their conventions should be adhered to. The beach and adjacent streets are one thing, but the rest of the island is very much another.

It's particularly important to wear reasonably formal dress when visiting government offices. This may differ from what's considered formal back home, and you should simply look at what the better-off Indonesians wear to get an idea of their expectations of you. Short sleeves, for instance, are perfectly acceptable for men, and ties are rare. But long trousers, shoes as opposed to sandals or thongs, and above all a neat, newly pressed general appearance are essential ingredients of the style.

For women, modesty is the keynote. Remember that it's going to be hot, and sometimes very hot, and that loose-fitting clothes are much cooler than close-fitting ones. Cotton is also cooler than artificial fabrics.

To enter a Balinese temple, one must wear a sarong and a sash. Most will rent these for a fee, but it is simpler to buy them for a few thousand rupiah and carry them with you.

A moment's thought is worth pages of advice. You would never dream of turning up to a funeral at home in beachwear, but it's astonishing how many tourists turn up in shorts and a T-shirt to a Balinese cremation.

BARGAINING

Be prepared to bargain for most things in Bali. It's the most natural, and surely the most ancient, system in the world. If you want to buy, and he wants to sell, why should anything as rigid as a fixed price come between you?

You can even bargain for your hotel room, along the lines of "What price will you give me if I stay a week?" or "What's the discount, seeing as it is low season?" It may turn out to be inappropriate, but it's necessary to understand the Balinese will never be surprised — to them, it's fixed prices that are unnatural, the foreign importation.

The secret of successful bargaining is to get your offer in first. Once the vendor has named a price, it would involve too much loss of face to accept anything much less than sixty percent of it. Nevertheless, for you to make the first offer, and then go on to describe it immediately as your last price, is to go against the whole spirit of the business, and is guaranteed to remove the smile off any Indonesian face. You've simply broken the rules, and been very rude in the bargain because you've left him no room to maneuver.

There are places, though, where you don't bargain — restaurants and the larger shops for instance. And the Balinese don't bargain over bemo fares, though you might find yourself having to if you haven't managed to find out the correct fare in advance. But wherever you're dealing with someone who's master of his own business, whether it's a girl hawking T-shirts on the beach or a boy offering to drive you around on the back of his motorbike, bargaining is the accepted, and expected, way to go about things.

Also, remember this is a culture where sellers frequently approach you with their wares. This often annoys visitors, on Kuta Beach for example, but remember that any answer, even "No thanks," is often taken as an indication of at least some degree of interest. A silent shake of the head — and a smile — will normally see you aren't disturbed any longer.

OPPOSITE: Fishing *prahu* on the beach at Sanur. They will even take you across the Badung Strait to Jungutbatu on Nusa Lembongan — a trip that seems frightningly far for such simple craft.

TIPPING

Tipping isn't really the custom on Bali, but this shouldn't prevent you rewarding someone who has provided you with a useful service. You might, for example, tip your room boy after an extended stay but not after a short one. There's no need at all to tip in restaurants.

WATER SPORTS

SURFING

Surfing is a world all of its own. It's a religious cult with its own hermetic language and sacred locations.

Bali is considered one of the world's ideal surfing venues because of the consistency of its waves, breaking in exactly the same way for hours on end, and because when conditions make the ocean on one beach flat, there are other beaches only a short drive away where the surfing is likely to be stupendous.

The classic place for surfing is Ulu Watu. Here the waves are world class and surfing films and international competitions have been held here. Close by is Padang Padang. Neither venue is for the beginner, but both are well off the usual tourist routes and ideal for watching the masters of the art at play.

At Kuta the waves are smaller (though they can still be too dangerous to surf at all). Here, the classic locations are halfway between Kuta and Legian — "Half-Legian" — Kuta Reef, and Canggu and Medowi further north up the beach.

In addition, some surfers make the trip out to Nusa Lembongan, and, in the rainy season, surf off the reef at Sanur.

SAILING AND WINDSURFING

Sailing and windsurfing are available on the sheltered eastern side of the islands during the dry season. Inquire at any of the larger hotels at Nusa Dua or Sanur. For more reasonable rates than these are likely to offer you, ask along Sanur Beach, or at the Rai Restaurant at Benoa. Sailing is on local outriggers or the occasional Hobie Cat catamaran.

DIVING

There's superb diving on the remote island of Menjangan in the northwest. The Lovina beaches in North Bali have good snorkeling, and both snorkeling and diving are available on Nusa Lembongan.

Baruna, (51223; fax 53809 and **Bali Dolphin Divers, (** 27078 are two companies who will arrange everything for you.

RAFTING

Contact **Bali Adventure Rafting, (** 51292 or 54334, or **Sobek, (** 88498 or 87291; fax 88764, to participate in this new-to-Bali sport.

SAFETY IN SURF

Lives are lost every year on Bali's beaches. See the KUTA section (p.114) for details of the work of the Surf Rescue teams.

Remember — never go more than waist-deep unless you are a very strong swimmer. If a current is pulling you out to sea, don't try to swim against it, but sidewards out of it. And if in distress of any kind, raise a hand above your head — it's the international signal for help and represents your best chance of being rescued.

OTHER RELIGIONS

There are several churches and mosques in Denpasar, and in addition various large hotels hold services. Details are as follows:
Catholic
Churches
Jalan Kepundung, Denpasar.
St. Francis Xavier, Kuta/Tuban.
Services in hotels
Bali Beach Hotel, Legong Room, Saturday 5 pm.
Bali Hyatt, Hibiscus Room, Saturday 6 pm.
Bali Sol, Conference Hall I, Sunday 5 pm.
Nusa Dua Beach Hotel, Garuda Room, Sunday 6 pm

Protestant
Churches
Protestant Maranatha, Jalan Surapati, Denpasar.
Seventh Day Adventist, Jalan Surapati, Denpasar.
Pentecostal, Jalan Karna, Denpasar.
Services in hotels
Bali Beach Hotel, Sunday 6 pm.

Islamic
Mosques
Raya Mosque, Jalan Hasanudin, Denpasar.

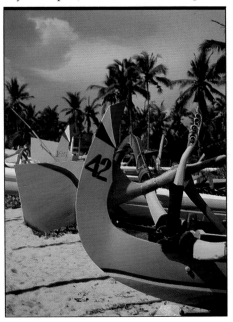

Annur Mosque, Jalan Diponegoro, Denpasar.
Taqwa Mosque, Jalan Supratman, Denpasar.
Services in hotels
Al-Hissan Mosque, Bali Beach Hotel.

ETIQUETTE

The Balinese are very polite and visitors should try to be the same.

A few simple points will see you a long way toward fitting in with their environment.

— Give and take everything with the right hand. The left is considered unclean.

— Never touch anyone on the head, even a child.

— Don't photograph people bathing in rivers, and in other circumstances ask first, if only with a smile and a gesture.

— Don't beckon someone toward you with your index finger as it's very rude.

— Wear a sash around your waist whenever you go into a temple, and at a ceremony such as a cremation don't wear shorts, thongs and a skimpy T-shirt. No one will be the slightest bit amused if you wear a sarong; they will be delighted, and many people will compliment you on your taste.

— Pointing at people, standing with your arms folded or with your hands on your hips are widely considered vulgar.

The Balinese, incidentally, rarely say "thank you" in the normal run of things on receipt of a gift. If they do so, it will be because they have been trained to do it by the hotel where they work. Similarly, it's impolite to call someone simply by his first name in Bali, but hotel workers have been trained to accept this slight along with other imported barbarisms.

SEX

Inevitably, male visitors will be offered prostitutes in Bali, especially in Kuta, but it is to the eternal credit of the Balinese that they will very rarely be from Bali itself. Touts will whisper "Balinese girl, very young" to you on a dark night, but they will almost certainly be from one of the other islands and the touts are confident no foreigner will ever know the difference.

LANGUAGE

The language generally known as Bahasa Indonesia ("the Indonesian language") is actually Malay. The language of Bali is Balinese, a difficult tongue with different forms for addressing the various social classes. All Balinese now learn Bahasa Indonesia in school, and as it is very easy, and can be used throughout Indonesia as well as in Malaysia, it's the one you should try to master at least a few phrases of. There

are no articles, no plurals, and no tenses, and the verb "to be" isn't used (Bali bagus = Bali is beautiful).

Pronunciation is easy and straightforward: the important point is that Indonesian is easy to *hear*. Most people can pick up the sounds and general intonation parrot-like almost at once. In this, Indonesian contrasts strongly with most other Asian languages which, with their complex systems of tones, are very difficult.

Because it's so easy, it's immense fun to try. It's also very poetic. Start off with some of the following:

Good Morning. *Selamat pagi.* ("May your action be blessed this morning.")

How are you? *Apa khabar?* ("What's the news?")

I'm fine. *Khabar baik.* ("The news is good.")

Thank you. *Terima kasih.*

It's a pleasure. *Kembali.*

Goodbye (when *you're* leaving). *Permisi.* (The reply to this is *Mari*.)

What is your name? *Siapa namamu?*

My name is ... *Nama saya...*

Please speak slowly. *Tolong bicara pelan-pelan.*

I'll come back later. *Saya akan kembali nanti.*

May I come in? *Boleh saya masuk?*

This is good! *Ini bagus!*

Is it safe to swim here? *Anam berenang disini?*

How much is this? *Berapa haga ini?*

About... *Kira kira...*

1, 2, 3, 4, 5... *Satu, dua, tiga, empat, lima...*

...6, 7, 8, 9, 10. ...*enam, tujuh, delapan, sembilan, sepuluh.*

11, 12, 13... *sebelas, dua belas, tiga belas* (*belas* = ten)

20, 30... *dua puluh, tiga puluh* (*puluh* = tens)

100 *seratus*

200, 300... *dua ratus, tiga ratus* (*ratus* = hundreds)

1,000 *seribu*

2,000, 3,000... *dua ribu, tiga ribu* (*ribu* = thousands)

100,000 *seratus ribu*

And in answer to the eternal question "Where are you going?" try "*Makan angin*" ("To eat the wind").

A helpful little booklet is John *Barker's Practical Indonesian*, available all over Bali.

CONSULATES AND EMBASSIES

Eight countries maintain consulates, consular agencies, representatives or honorary consuls in Bali. They are:

Australia Jalan Raya Sanur, Tanjung Bungkak, Denpasar, (35092.
France Jalan Raya Sesetan 46d, Banjar Pesanggaran, Denpasar, (33555.
Germany Jalan Pantai Karang 17, Sanur, (88826.
Italy Jalan Cemara, Banjar Semawang, Sanur, (88896 and 88996.
Japan Jalan Moh. Yamin 9 — Renon, Denpasar, (34808.
Sweden c/o Hotel Segara Village, Sanur, (88408.
Switzerland c/o Swiss Restaurant, Jalan Pura Bagus Taruna, Legian, Kuta, (51735.
United States Jalan Segara Ayu 5, Sanur, (88478.
UK citizens should apply to the Australian Consul and **Finnish** citizens to the Swedish Consul. Other nationals may be able to get advice from one of the above, or they can contact their own embassy in Jakarta.

The following are the phone numbers of the various embassies in Jakarta:
Afghanistan, (33169/342677.
Algeria, (49310/352694.
Argentina, (45368/338088.
Australia, (23109/331856.
Austria, (45811/248568.
Bangladesh, (21690/324850.
Belgium, (48719/351682.
Bolivia, (21362.
Brazil, (58378.
Brunei, (583051 ext 1613.
Bulgaria, (43926/346725.
Burma, (20440/327204.
Canada, (584031
Chile, (584309/587611.
Columbia, (517717/516446.
Czechoslovakia, (40538/344994.
Denmark, (48615.
Egypt, (45325/345572.
Finland, (516980.
France, (32807/332403.
Germany, (882414/882491
Hungary, (587521/587522.

India, (581850/588182.
Iran, (31391.
Iraq, (55016/355017.
Italy, (47907/348339.
Japan, (24308.
Kampuchea, (467836.
Malaysia, (32864/336647.
Mexico, (33909/337974.
New Zealand, (30620/330680.
North Korea, (46457.
Norway, (54556/354557.
Pakistan, (50576/350577.
Panama, (41995.
Papua New Guinea, (584604.
Philippines, (46786.
Poland, (20509.
Portugal, (54521/365111.
Romania, (49524.
Saudi Arabia, (46342.
Singapore, (48761.
South Korea, (58081/512309.
Spain, (25996.
Sweden, (32306/333061.
Switzerland, (517468.
Syria, (44334/354570.
Thailand, (43762/348221.
Turkey, (36809.
United Kingdom, (30904/331039.
United States, (60360.
Russia, (21477.
Vatican, (41142.
Vietnam, (47325.
Yemen, (45225.
Yugoslavia, (33720.

SELECTED INDONESIAN MISSIONS ABROAD

Australia
Canberra, (73-3222.
Darwin, (819352.
Melbourne, (6907811.
Perth, (219821.
Sydney, (264-2976/2195/2323.
Austria
Vienna, (342533/4/5.
Belgium
Brussels, (771-2013/4.
Canada
Ontario, (236-7403/5.
Toronto, (5916613/5916461.
Vancouver, (682-8855/8.

Denmark
Copenhagen, (624422 / 625439.
France
Paris, (2881999.
Marseilles, (713435.
Germany
Bonn, (310091.
Dusseldorf, (353081.
Frankfurt, (231740.
Hannover, (1032150.
Munich, (294609.
Greece
Athens, (8814082.
Hong Kong, (7904421/8.
India
Delhi, (602352/602343/ 602308.
Italy
Rome, (475-9251/2/3.
Japan
Tokyo, (441-4201-9.
Kobe, (321-1654.
Sapporo, (251-6602.
Malaysia
Kuala Lumpur, (421011/421141/ 421228/421354/421460.

New Zealand
Wellington, (758695/9.
Netherlands
The Hague, (469796.
Singapore (7377422.
South Korea
Seoul, (782-5116/8.
Spain
Madrid, (4130294/4130594.
Switzerland
Bern, (440983/5.
Thailand
Bangkok, (2523125/2523177.
United Kingdom
London, (499-7661.
USA
Washington DC, (293-1745.
Chicago, (938-0101.
Honolulu, (524-4300.
Houston, (626-3291.
Los Angeles, (383-5126/8.
New York, (879-0600.
San Francisco, (474-9571.

The enjoyment is evident as these girls proceed to a purification ceremony on Kuta Beach.

Bibliography

BAUM, Vicki A *Tale from Bali* (1937). Reissued in paperback by OUP. Translated from German, a novel set between 1904 and 1906 when the Dutch were extending their control over the island.

COVARRUBIAS, Miguel *The Island of Bali* (1937). Reissued in paperback by OUP. The classic account. Essentially a systematic survey of Balinese life and culture interspersed with personal recollections from this Mexican painter who made two extended visits to the island.

DALTON, Bill *Indonesia Handbook* (2nd edn 1980). Moon Publications, Chico, Ca. Though ostensibly for the back-packing budget traveler, this voluminous and outspoken account has, almost despite itself, reached classic status. Inevitably lacking detail on Bali, it is the guidebook to take with you to the rest of Indonesia.

EISEMAN, Fred B. *Bali, Sekala and Niskala* (2 vols, 1985, 1986). The leading authority on everything Balinese, Eiseman is a retired American academic chemist who spends six months of every year on Bali. These two books, contain a vast range of information on everything from Balinese scripts (which Eiseman is computerizing) to the manufacture of concrete telephone poles on the Bukit. Breathtaking.

EISEMAN, Margaret and Fred *Flowers of Bali* (1987). An identification aid to some of the commoner flowers of the island, with color photographs.

KERTONEGORO, Madi *The Spirit Journey to Bali Aga, Tenganan Pegringsingan* (1986). Harkat Foundation, Bali. A whimsical, eccentric but amusing account of some legends from the Candi Dasa/Tenganan area.

KOCH, C.J. *The Year of Living Dangerously* (1978). Reissued by Grafton paperbacks. An imaginative and sympathetic novel set in Jakarta at the time of the fall of Sukarno in 1965. An enormously interesting insight into Indonesian life and politics.

LEURAS, Leonard, and LLOYD, Ian R. *Bali, the Ultimate Island* (1987). Times Editions. The ultimate Bali picture-book, with additional photographs by Cartier-Bresson and other old masters.

MABBETT, Hugh *In Praise of Kuta* (1987). January Books, Wellington. Breaking with the "cultural treasurehouse" tradition, this is a collection of short essays on Bali's much-maligned tourist capital.

MATHEWS, Anna *The Night of Purnama* (1965). Reissued in paperback by OUP. A low-key account of living in the village of Iseh, north of Klungkung, culminating in the eruption of nearby Agung in 1963.

MAY, Brian *The Indonesian Tragedy* (1978) RKP, London and Boston. An in-depth, but also personal, look at modern Indonesian politics from a journalist who worked for many years in the country. Disenchanted but passionate. A surprisingly good read.

McPHEE, Colin *A House in Bali* (1947). Reissued by OUP in Oxford in Asia paperback series. McPhee was an American composer who went to Bali to study the gamelan (which he describes as "a shining rain of silver"). The first Westerner to build a house at Kuta, his book is sensitive and intelligent.

POWELL, Hickman *The Last Paradise* (1930). Reissued in paperback by OUP. One of the very early books. Rather specifically American, it is by turns sardonic and lushly poetic. Describes the gamelan as "the muffled laughter of forgotten gods." Richly readable.

RAMSEYER, Urs *The Art and Culture of Bali* (1977). Fribourg. Translated from German, a quasi-academic survey. Rather like a vast museum catalogue with innumerable black-and-white photographs. Dispensable.

TANTRI, K'tut *Revolt in Paradise*. Reissued in Indonesia, in English, Indonesian and Dutch, by Gramedia Paperbacks. A high-spirited account of the adventures of a young American woman who went to Bali alone in the 1930s, helped set up Kuta's first hotel, was imprisoned by the Japanese, and became famous throughout the region as "Surabaya Sue", freedom-fighter with the Indonesians. Born Vannine Walker, her original pseudonym was Muriel Pearson.

Limited to only five books, I'd take Koch, Powell, May, Covarrubias, and McPhee, and get hold of Eiseman and Tantri when I got to Bali.

Quick Reference A–Z Guide
to Places and Topics of Interest with Listed Accommodation, Restaurants and Useful Telephone Numbers

Illustrated Blueprints to Travel Enjoyment

INSIDER'S
GUIDES

The Guides That Lead